CIP catalogue record of this title is available from the South African
Library

ISBN: 978-0-7961-7911-1

Disclaimer

This book provides educational information and is not intended as
personalised advice· The content reflects the views of the author,
Avril A Williamson, and is believed to be accurate· However, it is not
tailored to individual educational or HR developmental needs· Past
results do not guarantee future performance· This book should not
be used as the sole basis for HR decisions· No warranty is made
regarding the accuracy or completeness of the information· The
author disclaims any liability for any loss or risk incurred, directly or
indirectly, from the use or application of the book's contents·

Email: avril@thepeoplepractices·com

Website: https://thepeoplepractices·com

First Published in 2025 by The People Practices

Cover Design by News Creative

Dedication

This book is dedicated to my family and friends, for their unwavering support throughout my career as an HR professional.

I also dedicate this work to HR Executives and HR Professionals who are passionate about people and tirelessly advocate for and promote the positive aspects of the HR profession.

Preamble

As a global community of dedicated Human Resources professionals, we come from diverse backgrounds yet share a common goal: to deliver and sustain an exceptional employee experience within the workplace for great organisational outcomes and results. Our collective voice surely echoes a shared sentiment.

It is a privilege to be HR professionals, so let's continue this fascinating journey together and unpack what some experienced Human Resources Professionals are saying and doing.

In essence, The People to Profit HR Practice Code is all about driving the implementation of exceptional employee experiences to achieve this outcome:

Happier HR Professionals = Happier Employees = Happier Customers = Greater Company Profits.

So, the framework that supports you to get there is The People to Profit HR Practice Code, which is all about championing the implementation of great employee experiences.

Now, let's dive in, master this practice code, and transform ourselves and our people we serve for greater success!

Introduction and Overview

Gear Up for a More Meaningful Contribution
Through the People to Profit Practice HR Code

Welcome to *The People to Profit HR Practice Code™*, a unique journey that redefines HR practices and focuses on creating a more human-centered approach in the workplace. This book empowers HR professionals to transform their practices, blending compassion and strategic insight to drive business success.

Unlike traditional HR books, this book offers a transformative experience to an HR Leader and Professional, with a mix of practical HR tools with uplifting, soul-inspiring wisdom. It aims to help HR professionals overcome common challenges such as talent acquisition and retention, compliance and legal risks, and especially maintaining high employee engagement and morale levels. These challenges are crucial to organisational success and demand proactive strategies and adaptation, to especially deliver a great employee experience.

However, I must emphasise that the real gap in HR is the failure to recognise the full value people bring when their experience is truly enhanced. To achieve greater business results and profits, employee engagement must extend beyond satisfaction to creating a meaningful experience that fosters growth for the HR Professional, the employee and the company. In my opinion, this enhancement of the employee experience for both personal and business growth is what should truly keep Chief HR executives awake at night.

Employee engagement, when combined with a focus on employee experience, represents a powerful business strategy that is scalable for several reasons:

- Enhancing the employee experience leads to higher productivity, greater innovation, and stronger alignment with organisational goals. In other words impact on performance is greater.

- It also reduces turnover costs, fosters a positive workplace culture, and makes companies more attractive to top talent, supporting long-term scalability. This derives cost savings for a company.

- Scalable engagement strategies are effective across industries and organisations of all sizes, leveraging technology to gather insights, measure impact, and drive continuous improvement. This means it is applicably broad.

- Investing in employee engagement fosters loyalty, resilience, and sustainable growth, giving businesses a competitive edge. Great long-term impact.
- Consulting, training, and data-driven approaches further ensure measurable outcomes, demonstrating a clear return on investment in the employee experience.

While Talent Acquisition and Retention, along with Compliance and Legal Risks, are critical business priorities, focusing on Employee Engagement and delivering great Employee Experiences offers scalable opportunities to enhance organisational performance, attract top talent, and foster a positive workplace culture across industries. So, get ready for a journey that will reshape the HR world, one smile at a time! Prepare to step beyond your comfort zone as this transformative experience empowers you to elevate both yourself and your HR practice, unlocking lasting rewards along the way.

As a corporate HR leader, you may be worried that your business isn't fully prioritising the human capital strategy, which could **maybe** limit your ability to achieve **performance goals,** especially when it comes to improving both employee and customer experiences for greater profitability.

You may **possibly** feel that others don't fully recognise **HR's impact** in shaping positive employee experiences that drive business success, which misses the opportunity for the company to thrive even more with HR's contributions. **Possibly,** you are also a Chief HR Executive facing the challenge of having to enhance the **employee experience** to drive both **employee and business growth.** Without a strong focus on this, we know that organisations risk disengagement, higher turnover, and unrealised potential, making it a critical issue that demands attention. You may **potentially** want to gain greater **confidence in showcasing** HR's value to the business to secure leadership buy-in, influence strategic decisions, and demonstrate HR's direct impact on business success. With greater confidence, you can **effectively advocate for initiatives that enhance employee engagement,** drive performance, and contribute to profitability, ensuring HR is recognised as a key driver of organisational growth. **Perhaps** you've inherited a toxic workplace culture, resulting in disengaged employees and an unhealthy environment, leaving you concerned about the potential reputational damage to the company. Additionally, attracting and retaining skilled talent may be challenging, with high turnover affecting both performance and financial stability.

But imagine overcoming these challenges and becoming recognised as a professional and leader who champions employee engagement and experiences. This means that you would play a key role in driving positive changes, with a clear vision for the future and a spotlight on your contributions during the company's strategic business leadership engagements.

This change is an invitation to have a mindset shift where better employee experiences are made accessible to all people in an organisation, whilst getting to know and understand the **Essence of People** and what needs to be done to Support the Business more. My hope is that it will inspire and ignite your passion to create an even greater positive organisational impact as an HR professional and Executive and that you will make an even greater contribution to the growth of the HR profession.

I also wish for you to be intentional and to elevate your HR practice through an offering that provides a great engagement and employee experience, and it all begins with connecting with ourselves as professionals and then connecting with people, as people connect with people to leverage their maximum potential to provide an even better employee experience. As the intention is to direct a happier workforce and workplace, for greater results and profits. So, let's wrap it up with this simple code to keep in your back pocket!

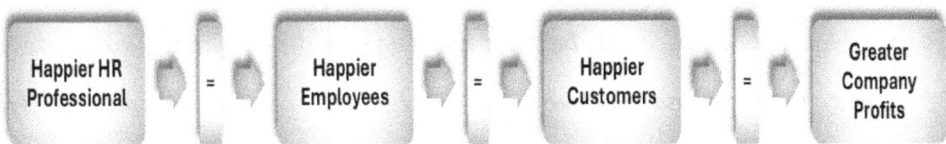

Happier HR Professional = Happier Employees = Happier Customers = Greater Company Profits

Our journey together to activate and implement a superior HR Practice will cover five key pillar areas:

Pillar 1: _Equip:_ **Establishing the foundational fundamentals through sound Protocols.**

HR professionals can sometimes fall into the trap of just being themselves, without fully tapping into the deeper essence of what it means to be human. When this happens, they may miss the opportunity to truly harness human potential in a way that fosters both personal growth and the company's success. It's about embracing who we all are as people and using that understanding to drive prosperity and positive change within the organisation.

The People to Profit Practice Code™ helps you to know and understand the foundational fundamental basics within the HR Profession and what it means to be **human**. The same goes for all HR professionals, it's equally important for CHROs, Chief People Officers and Executives, managers, and business partners too. Everyone has a role to play in embracing the foundational basics and driving meaningful change within the organisation. To do this successfully, you need to know and understand yourself and others around you better through a heightened **awareness**. In this understanding, you need to be confident as an HR Professional. This is as an invitation for every HR professional to act with intentionality, observation, outlook, and opinion, where they have the knowledge and where they advise creatively with curiosity and intuition in an **Uplifting Way.**

So, every HR professional would need to be **Aware** of their own being (self) and of those that they serve (Others); they would need to **Consciously Commit** to the profession and engage with the business in transforming theirs and the business beliefs, and would need to be exemplary in the **Treatment** of themselves and others by ensuring that they have the necessary skills and provide the proper HR **Standards** to enhance the employee experience. This needs to be undertaken in an uplifting way. This is cardinal for HR Professionals if they want to achieve exceptional employee and customer experience for the company. Professional individual capability levels are assessed by the HR professionals and by the business leaders they serve in terms of the value that they bring to the employees and the company leadership.

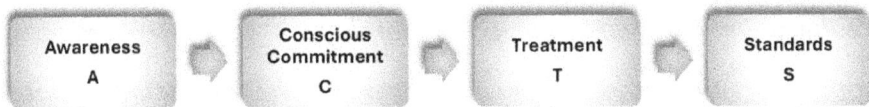

Awareness A		Conscious Commitment C		Treatment T		Standards S

These 4 foundational elements give the HR professionals a superhero cape, allowing them to take charge with purpose, creativity, and integrity.

Pillar 2: <u>Empower</u>: Activating best-in-class HR Practices to enhance the employee engagement experience.

*The second dimension an HR professional must master is how to **activate a superior HR practice**. To drive immediate business impact, HR professionals need to establish their practice swiftly by identifying and implementing high-value HR interventions and solutions **at every employee touchpoint**.*

*Let's take a moment to explore the process behind this **activation**. Here the HR professionals align their practices with the company's business cycle, strategic milestones, and employee interactions.*

*The process begins with defining the **goal that is** the "why" behind the effort and what needs to be done to achieve meaningful results for the company. Next comes the **game plan**, addressing the "what" and "when" by mapping out a strategic roadmap. This plan pinpoints the HR areas with the greatest impact, ensuring both employees and the company **gain** from an enhanced experience that drives satisfaction and business success. Throughout the journey, ongoing **guidance** provides the "how," offering clarity, direction, and support for seamless execution and long-term **growth**. So, **growth** is central to both personal development and the overall success of the business.*

The key principle of "**there is no growth of business without growth of people**" underscores this idea. As employees grow in their skills, knowledge, and engagement, the business naturally benefits through improved performance, innovation, and adaptability.

By fostering individual growth, organisations empower their teams to contribute more effectively, driving the collective growth of the company and ensuring long-term success for both employees and the business.

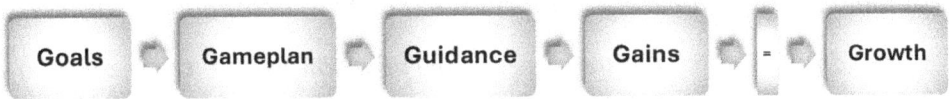

Goals → Gameplan → Guidance → Gains → = → Growth

By leveraging this second dimension through following these steps — activates a superior HR practice. It is essential for driving immediate and long-term business success.

As such HR Professionals can effectively align their strategies with the company's business cycle and key employee touchpoints. This approach not only enhances employee satisfaction but also contributes to the company overall performance and profitability.

Pillar 3: <u>Enable</u>: Creating a consistent image of growth by strategically positioning human resources.

*The Third key to excelling at creating a great employee experience is to **create a consistent image of growth,** not just for the people, but for the company. It's all too common for HR professionals to stay behind the scenes, working tirelessly in the background, rather than stepping into the spotlight to drive employee engagement. By focusing more on creating meaningful employee experiences, HR can clearly showcase how their efforts directly contribute to the company's success and bottom line. It's time for HR Professionals to take on a more visible role and highlight the positive impact they make on the business. Creating a consistent image of growth is done by putting The People to Profit Pathway into action. This means that HR Professionals need to understand the link between People and Profit as its about optimising human capital to drive profitability and business success, through the growth of both the people and the business.*

*The essential elements that would assist an HR professional to **Position** Human Resources to direct and create the possibility of a happier workplace include:*

- *the **professionalism** of HR, which underscores the importance of HR's expertise and ethical conduct,*

- the **power** of HR, highlighting its influence in shaping culture,
- the **promotion** of HR, ensuring its role is visible and valued across the business,
- the **products** of HR, focusing on the tools and services HR delivers,
- the **packaging** of HR, which is about how these services are presented and implemented, and finally,
- the **profit** contribution of HR, showing how HR directly impacts the financial success of the organisation.

Following these steps is crucial for strategically positioning HR to maximize impact and drive business success.

4. _Engage:_ Leveraging the power of human resources' voice for valuable appropriate engagement, through the art of presenting.

HR professionals must **leverage their V·O·I·C·E·** to enhance engagement and deliver impactful presentations with ease. This requires a structured presentation system that ensures clear, compelling communication while keeping the audience engaged, all in a stress-free way.

It begins with looking at voice **Variety,** using modulation, adjusting pitch, and being mindful of your stance and personal delivery. This means changing up your tone and style to keep things interesting and dynamic. It's an approach that wants your voice to reflect not just the words you're saying but the emotion and importance behind them. This you accomplish by optimising your voice so be aware of the acoustics and the size of your audience, adjusting your volume so everyone can hear you clearly. It's important to project confidence and clarity, no matter the size of the crowd.

Intonation plays a key role in conveying meaning and emphasis to your message. By varying your tone, you can highlight important points and keep the flow of your speech smooth and engaging. Intonation helps your audience understand when you're shifting topics, asking questions, or making key points.

Clarity is essential in making sure your message is easily understood, articulated, structured for the audience to follow your storyline without confusion. As a well organised message is more likely to leave a lasting impact.

Lastly, **engagement** comes through connecting with your audience. Use movement and eye contact to maintain their attention, and ensure your voice is not just heard but felt.

This combination of techniques helps make your message more memorable and impactful.

An HR Professional learns the skills of delivering a compelling, believable, engaging presentation that will give them the confidence to present in a public setting through storytelling, in a way that captivates and inspires the client to buy into the recommended human resources solutions and interventions. This gives the Human Resources professional the opportunity to better position themselves on their offering.

Additionally, an HR Professional who is more confident in public speaking and storytelling is better equipped to negotiate, foster partnerships and secure resources for their department which directly translates into financial benefits for the business.

This is especially important when trying to position HR as a critical business driver that contributes to profitability of the organisation.

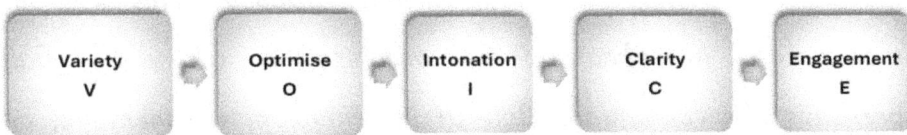

Variety	Optimise	Intonation	Clarity	Engagement
V	O	I	C	E

It is critical for HR professionals looking to elevate their presentations and engage their audience to follow through in a way that leaves a lasting impact.

Pillar 5: _Elevate_: Advocating and Advancing Great HR Practices through effective Partnership and Promotion.

We promote the implementation of great HR practices to enhance Employee **Experience**, boost performance, and elevate company results.

So, this final dimension empowers HR professionals to **advance** their practice by advocating a **win-and-grow game plan** through the strategic **promotion** of HR. This is achieved by leveraging:

- Effective Tools

- Impactful interventions and Initiatives and

- Referring to HR Practice Notes

By championing these elements, HR professionals can **elevate their influence** and drive meaningful organisational success. This, in turn, strengthens the **HR value proposition,** the unique benefits and advantages an organisation offers its employees, while demonstrating **ROI and business impact.** This approach serves as the **heartbeat of the organisation**, where the pulse represents the continuous flow of information, engagement, and strategic alignment. Just as a healthy heart circulates oxygen and nutrients to sustain life, a strong people-centric approach fuels employee engagement and productivity, driving a significant return on investment. The rhythm of this **heartbeat** reflects the organisation's vitality, ensuring that every investment in talent and culture delivers measurable benefits and contributes to financial growth.

This approach empowers HR professionals to design and implement targeted interventions and solutions that align with business needs, driving meaningful results. In essence, it answers three key questions:

Where is the business now? Where does it want to be? And how can HR bridge the gap to achieve greater profitability?

This approach enhances the **skills, confidence, and expertise** of HR professionals, equipping them to **elevate the fundamentals of a strong HR practice.** By leveraging **HR Practice Notes** as a starting point, HR professionals can evolve, add value, and drive business growth, creating a **strategic partnership** where company goals are achieved more effectively.

The 5 elements of **Promote:**

Partner	→	Provide	→	Pitch	→	Practice	→	Perform

First, there's **Partner,** this is where you focus on influencing and collaborating to achieve a common goal that benefits everyone. By building strong partnerships, you can tap into shared resources and ideas, making the journey to success a team effort. Next is **Provide**. This is about offering something valuable that others need or want. Whether it's resources, support, or expertise, when you provide what's essential, you're helping to move things forward.

Then comes **Pitch** This is your moment to shine where your ideas, products, or services are presented in a way that persuades others to support or buy into what you're offering. A compelling pitch can win over hearts and minds. **Practice** to win is all about honing your skills. Engaging in activities that improve your proficiency and provide you with the know how to implement the HR Practice notes to make you even better at what you do. The more you practice, the more prepared you are to seize challenges and opportunities and still succeed.

Finally, there's **Perform**. This is where you deliver on your promises and focus on achieving results. It's about following through and ensuring that your efforts lead to the outcomes you're aiming for. In promoting Human Resources, this approach fosters **collaboration** to identify and close gaps, ensuring organisational success. By applying the **five key dynamic elements** of Partnering, Providing, Pitching, Practicing and Performing, HR professionals can effectively showcase HR's value. Through **HR Practice Notes**, they can also reference relevant **HR metrics** that demonstrate **ROI** by linking HR initiatives directly to business performance and profitability. This holistic approach ensures HR professionals **win and grow**, driving sustainable success for both employees and the organisations, thereby giving **HR the Edge.**

In conclusion, each of these pillars of Protocol, Practices, Position, Present, and Promote is essential for achieving success in any venture, transforming collaboration into tangible results. By being equipped, empowered, enabled, engaged, and elevated, HR professionals are prepared to make a lasting impact.

As a result, HR professionals are positioned to consistently deliver meaningful contributions, leading to:

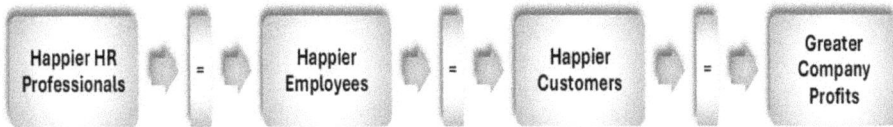

Happier HR Professionals = Happier Employees = Happier Customers = Greater Company Profits

By mastering these 5 pillars, HR professionals can consistently deliver **meaningful contributions**, leading to **Stronger Employee Engagement** through creating a motivated and high-performing workforce, **Enhanced Business Performance** by Aligning HR strategies with organisational goals for measurable success, **Increased Retention and Talent Growth** through fostering a workplace that attracts and retains top talent, **improved HR Credibility and Influence** by positioning HR as a key driver of business strategy. and **Greater Return on Investment (ROI)** by demonstrating the tangible impact of HR initiatives on profitability. By staying ahead of the curve and embracing innovation, Human Resources professionals can effectively support organisational goals and foster a successful workplace culture to drive greater profits.

So, as you embark on this transformative journey it will ultimately lead you to being a more confident happier professional.

Chapter One

A Journey to Conscious Commitment
Through Harnessing the Human Element

Show up as an Expert Partner from the Onset

The essence of who we are as human beings is made up of the essential characteristics that define our identity and our existence, which are reflected in our minds, our hearts and our hands. that to which I refer to as being our **crown**, (head) **core** (heart), and **contribution** (hands).

We would, therefore, be remiss on our part not to engage on the meaning of the word human as it appears in the naming of our profession, that being "Human" Resources. Knowing and understanding what this truly means is essential as it would help our profession to achieve more, and our profession can also be viewed more correctly through the lenses of our fellow professions and in particular those that we are meant to work with.

In the workplace, the vitalness of being human often, referenced as human capacity, human capability, human capital, and human ability forms the basis and is key in the differentiation of successful companies. In South Africa, where I am from, we have called this notion of being human "Ubuntu." As this also extends to how you accept and engage with others in their humanness.

People are seen as the company's greatest asset, and being recognised and harnessing this human potential is essential to fostering growth, innovation, and prosperity in a company or organisation and even in society. Investing in human resources is therefore crucial for organisational success as it fosters employee engagement, enhances skills and capabilities, promotes innovation, and leads to improved performance and company outcomes.

Companies that develop these critical human elements through investing in their people achieve sustainable success and competitive advantage. So, within the organisation, HR Professionals have a great part to play in nurturing and growing people as at, its basic core is our 'humanness' and 'humaneness.' So, what do I mean by this?

I mean that being human is about the continuous process of growth, learning, adaptation, and the pursuit of fulfilment and well-being, that can also assist companies to drive productivity, innovation, and economic growth. This innate desire holds true for an HR professional as well. Our job isn't just to enforce rules or manage processes; it's about truly understanding the people we work with, their unique experiences, and the personal stories that shape their viewpoints.

As human beings, we can also awaken the power of our minds, as this involves harnessing our cognitive abilities, emotional intelligence, and mindset to achieve our goals, solve problems, and lead fulfilling lives. Investing in people is fundamentally a call for all to return to being human and tap into the abilities, skills, creativity, and motivation of people to achieve collective goals for the ultimate best employee experience, customer experience and company success.

As HR professionals, we are equally all human beings who have developed a mindset and core beliefs that are deeply held, which inform how we see ourselves and others in the world of work. So, beliefs are a subjective attitude or a mental state of having some stance, where we take an opinion about something in the world that is either true or false. The notion of core beliefs is central to a person's cognitive behaviour and core beliefs can either be helpful or unhelpful.

Professionally our collective beliefs arise when we have a joint commitment or acceptance of a certain belief. Beliefs are not easy to change and, as such, take time to do so. Where beliefs are unhelpful or unrealistic they may impact on a person's overall life or professional satisfaction. When it comes to being effective in HR, one of the most important things we can do is acknowledge the complexity of people's beliefs and experiences.

Recently, I had a conversation with someone whose beliefs were completely different from my own. At first, I was taken aback by their perspective, but as they shared more about their childhood and the experiences that shaped their worldview, I began to understand where they were coming from. This moment was a powerful reminder that many of our deepest beliefs aren't formed overnight, they're often rooted in our life experiences, the lessons passed down from our families, and the environments we've been part of.

As HR professionals, we too hold beliefs about ourselves and our roles. These beliefs influence how we approach our work and the impact we have within an organisation. If we see HR as purely an administrative function focused on tasks like payroll and compliance, we may miss out on the opportunity to contribute to the broader strategic goals of the company. But when we challenge our own assumptions and recognise the value we bring, we can position ourselves as key players in driving business success.

To truly understand others, we first need to reflect on our own beliefs. What do we believe about ourselves as HR professionals? How have our experiences shaped those beliefs? And are we open to evolving those views? By being introspective, we can challenge our limiting beliefs, embrace new ways of thinking, and ultimately become more effective in our roles. As HR professionals, the more we grow in our understanding of ourselves and others, the better we can serve our organisations and create positive, lasting change.

The essential characteristics that define our identity are reflected in our **crown,** (head) **core** (heart) and **contribution** (hands). And what do I mean by this? I mean that it relates to our heads and what we think about in our minds, what we feel in our hearts and how through our hands we contribute. These essential characteristics are also linked to our core beliefs.

There are, however, some fundamental beliefs that lie at the core of a successful HR Professional in practice and these also relate to us being human ourselves:

- Know right from wrong.
- Make decisions for the greater good of all human capital or in the best interest of both the employee and the employer.

- Treat everyone with the same respect/decorum and resolve matters at the individual and company level.
- Align what you think, say and do for a fair, unbiased ethical decision or response in every situation

As such, these beliefs ignite and fuel our conscious commitment

A successful HR Professional's approach to changing a belief, especially ones that can be deemed to be negative or non-value adding and which often lead to pains can be achieved by practising the following:

- Identify the belief you want to change by understanding why you hold that belief and how it impacts your life.
- Question and challenge the validity of the belief by examining evidence that supports or contradicts it and ask whether the belief is based on facts or assumptions.
- Educate yourself on the subject matter related to the belief by looking at different perspectives, research and experiences that may have alternative points of view.
- Replace limiting or negative beliefs with more empowering and positive ones where you focus on your well-being and personal growth.

- *Manage emotions that may be tied to certain beliefs through practising mindfulness and emotional regulation techniques to respond to challenging situations in a balanced and rational manner.*

- *Surround yourself with supportive persons who encourage personal growth and challenge limiting beliefs. Mentors, counsellors, coaches, and support groups can provide the necessary guidance.*

- *Be self-compassionate throughout the process of changing beliefs by recognising that it takes time and effort to rewire deeply ingrained patterns of thinking. So, you have the ability to create a belief at any time that you know would serve you well. You can therefore choose to change your belief in a moment.*

So, most importantly, you have the ability to create a belief at any time that you know would serve you better.

Let us consider an HR professional named David who initially struggled with treating everyone with fairness and the same level of respect. David used to believe that employees in certain positions or departments deserved more respect or attention than others based on their perceived importance to the organisation.

However, David's perspective began to shift when he encountered a situation involving a complaint from an employee in the maintenance department, let us call him Mark. Mark felt that he was unfairly treated compared to employees in other departments, especially those in managerial roles. He expressed frustration that his concerns were not being taken seriously and that he was often overlooked in favor of other departments. You therefore choose to change your belief in a moment!

Initially, David's instinct was to prioritise addressing issues raised by employees in higher-ranking positions or departments he perceived as more critical to the company's success. However, as he delved deeper into Mark's complaint and listened to his perspective, David realised the importance of treating everyone with fairness and respect, regardless of their role or department.

David made a conscious effort to address Mark's concerns promptly and with the same level of attention and respect he would afford to any other employee. He conducted a thorough investigation, listened empathetically to Mark's grievances and the outcomes that he sought, and took initiative-taking steps to address any underlying issues contributing to his dissatisfaction.

Through this experience, David learned the importance of recognising the value of every employee and treating them equally. He began to implement an approach that promoted fairness and equity across all levels of the organisation, fostering a culture where every employee felt valued and respected for their contributions and most importantly left experiencing an engagement that left them happier!

In the end, David's willingness to challenge his own beliefs and prioritise fairness and respect for all employees not only improved morale and satisfaction among the workforce but also strengthened the company's overall culture and company performance.

So, do HR professionals have beliefs about themselves that we need to reflect upon as they may need changing?

HR professionals, like individuals in any profession, may hold certain beliefs about themselves that could affect their effectiveness in their roles. Here are some examples:

Belief in HR's Role as Strictly to drive Administration: Some HR professionals may perceive their role primarily as administrative or transactional, focusing solely on tasks such as payroll, benefits administration, and record-keeping. While these tasks are essential, HR encompasses much more, including fostering a positive workplace culture. HR professionals who hold this belief may need to consider expanding their understanding of their role and embracing a more strategic and initiative-taking approach to HR management.

Belief in HR's Role as Policeman: In many organizations, HR professionals may be perceived as enforcers of company policies and procedures rather than as trusted advisors and advocates for employees. HR professionals who internalize this belief may adopt a compliance-focused mindset, prioritizing rule enforcement over employee support and development. To be effective, HR professionals should consider reframing their role as facilitators of employee success, promoting a culture of fairness, equity, and employee well-being.

Belief in HR's Limited Influence: Some HR professionals may believe that they have limited influence or authority within their organisation, especially if they report to higher-ranking executives or face resistance from other departments. This belief can lead to a lack of confidence and assertiveness in advocating for HR initiatives or addressing workplace issues. HR professionals may need to challenge this belief by recognizing the value they bring to the organisation and actively seeking opportunities to collaborate with leadership and other stakeholders to drive positive change.

Belief in HR's Lack of Influence on Organisational Strategy: Some HR professionals may believe that their role is disconnected from the broader organisational strategy and decision-making processes. They may see themselves as implementers rather than contributors to strategic planning and decision-making. HR professionals can challenge this belief by actively seeking opportunities to align HR initiatives with organisational goals, providing data-driven insights to inform decision-making, and positioning themselves as strategic partners to leadership.

By critically examining and potentially changing these beliefs, HR professionals can enhance their effectiveness, drive positive change within their organisations, and elevate the HR function as an enthusiastic strategic partner that contributes towards the achievement of organisational goals, thereby changing any overall negative views of HR that may exist.

1

Return to the Essence of Being Human and show up as a credible partner from the onset

---

HR professionals need to remember that changing beliefs is a gradual process that requires openness, innovative ideas, perseverance, and self-reflection as long as you remain committed to personal growth and self-improvement.

The essence of being human means possessing awareness as in **self-awareness** and an understanding of others, through rationality, one's conscious commitment and the capacity for empathy. Additionally, being human involves experiencing a range of emotions, forming relationships, pursuing goals and aspirations, and grappling with existential questions about meaning, purpose, and morality.

The problem I see is that some leaders and HR professionals take for granted the essence of being human or need to much more learn how to leverage human potential for overall individual and organisational success?

The challenge I see is that some HR leaders and HR professionals either overlook the essence of being human or need to better understand how to harness human potential to drive both individual and organisational success.

This means that both HR professionals, along with leadership and business, need to work jointly and collaboratively to **return to the essence of being human** especially when implementing HR Strategic objectives to unlock the full potential of their human capital and drive their organisational success by being more **aware**.

Start by **showing up as a credible partner right from the beginning** by implementing clear and reliable protocols. As an HR professional, it's crucial to first become fully **aware** of yourself, especially the value you bring and provide. i.e. your body, mind, soul, and overall well-being and sharpen your intuition by being more aware of those around you that you serve.

Next, it's about having a **Conscious Commitment** to your profession and your interactions with the business, aiming to positively transform both your own and the company's people beliefs.

2
Increase your self-awareness and the awareness of others around you

Lastly, you must exemplify excellent **Treatment,** both of yourself and others by ensuring you have the right skills and delivering high HR **Standards.** This will provide an employee experience that is not only efficient but one that happens in an uplifting and empowering way.

Awareness

Having the first foundational element of **protocols** in place regarding awareness can guide you in terms of how you should go about doing things in relation to your beliefs and mindset in the context of providing a tremendous human resource practice.

The fundamental principle for implementing a superior HR practice is to **increase** your self-awareness and the awareness of others around you.

The challenge I see *is* that many HR professionals start their practice without a strong foundation in self-awareness and awareness of others. As a result, they may struggle to fully understand their clients' needs, making it difficult to gain buy-in for the best HR practices and interventions. This lack of alignment can hinder business success, potentially leading to disengaged employees, lost customers, and missed opportunities for greater profitability.

Self-awareness involves recognising and understanding your abilities, talents, and positive traits that allow you to leverage your strengths in various aspects of your life, particularly your chosen profession. Being honest with yourself on your limitations and weaknesses. This awareness provides a foundation for understanding your unique "human" qualities, enabling you to navigate life with a deeper understanding of your capabilities and areas for growth. This awareness becomes a powerful tool for personal and professional development and success.

Here are some key reasons why being aware of others is essential:

- It enhances communication skills and builds stronger relationships as you understand others' needs, perspectives and emotions - so you have healthier connections with friends' family and colleagues.
- It assists you in understanding cultural differences and diversity. Being more highly socially aware also

creates an inclusive work environment. This also extends to providing employees and each other with good employment experiences, and in turn, excellent customer service and experience as you understand each other's needs, preferences, and concerns.

Therefore, the first step to resolving this problem is to become **aware**.

So, work on attaining a heightened innate awareness!

How can you heighten your awareness?

An excellent example of how this can be attained is by having a conversation with a business leader and finding out what keeps them awake at night? Once you have established this you can offer to work on a plan that would alleviate the named challenge by identifying the talented resources that are available to turn this around.

Another way is to conduct a self-assessment to better understand who you are as a person and get to know all the assessment outcomes of all those you serve. You will be well-positioned to identify the talented individuals who can make things happen and you will be great at advising on the basis that you will be playing the people to their strengths.

3 **Identify Talented** **Resources**

As a professional, having heightened awareness will allow you to tailor and refine your offerings to meet your customers' expectations better!

The challenge I see is that the strategic contributions HR professionals are expected to make often go unrealised due to gaps in awareness. Too often, HR services are not delivered at the individual level, leading to a lack of support for employees and leadership on critical people-related matters. This can manifest in customer complaints, disengaged employees, and poor business results.

To truly elevate their impact, HR professionals must develop the right mindset, as it serves as the foundation for how they provide services and implement interventions. A clear, growth-oriented mindset enables HR to drive meaningful change and steer the organisation forward. Since beliefs shape mindset, and mindset influences behaviors and outcomes, mastering one's mindset is essential for personal empowerment and professional excellence.

How should you develop a right mindset?

By tackling all your negative or false beliefs about yourself, your profession and those around you.

Conscious Commitment

4
Align your thoughts, words and actions

The second foundational element that a successful HR Professional aspires to is a clear and **conscious** dedicated **Commitment** to their profession and work, especially as it relates to their thoughts, words behaviours and actions.

It's a dedicated commitment to achieve the goals as set out. It involves making choices with a specific aim or objective in mind, with intentionality. This means that there is thought and purpose behind what one does, rather than actions being random or accidental.

In various contexts, there are behavioural intentions, cognitive intentions, and interpersonal intentions. Behavioural intentions are the deliberate actions or decisions someone makes with a specific goal or outcome in mind. Cognitive Intentions are the conscious thoughts or mental processes directed toward achieving a particular result. This includes commitment to work, setting goals and personal development. Interpersonal intentions are purposeful communication or actions taken with a clear objective in social interactions.

All thoughts, words and actions of a person need to be aligned so that they can be experienced as authentic and trustworthy!

In summary, the power of unleashing conscious commitment lies in its ability to drive focus, persistence, achievement, personal growth, trust, resilience, fulfilment, and inspiration.

HR Leaders and HR Professionals will need to talk about the importance of commitment as it relates to the various intentions in setting and achieving organisational goals. Overall, commitment involves a growth mindset and purpose-driven approach to decision-making.

5
Unlock your full potential to create a meaningful and lasting impact and have a growth mindset

By harnessing the power of commitment in various areas of work and life, you can unlock your full potential to create a meaningful and lasting impact.

A growth mindset emphasises the belief that abilities can be developed through effort and learning. Key aspects include embracing challenges, persisting in the face of setbacks, viewing failure as a learning opportunity, being open to feedback, admiring others' success, and cultivating resilience. It fosters a love of learning, resilience, and optimism, encouraging individuals to continuously seek growth and improvement.

Being aware of your mindset and your conscious commitment towards creating a positive environment for yourself and others is important, especially for an HR professional, as it shapes our experiences, our interactions and successes. Having a growth mindset as a practitioner is equally important as it fosters resilience and positive change, so shifting from a fixed mindset to a growth mindset is paramount.

Treatment

The third foundational element needed to be a successful professional is how you tackle, take care of, and firstly treat others. By this I mean that HR professionals need to be able to treat others with respect, compassion, and kindness, as it is essential for building positive relationships and fostering a healthy work environment. No matter how educated, fabulous or talented you believe you are, how you treat people tells it all. We're all familiar with the saying, "Treat others as you would want to be treated." This timeless principle is essential in fostering fairness, respect, and positive interactions with others. As human resources professionals play a crucial role in **Directing a Happy Workplace.**

What should HR professionals do to adopt a growth mindset?

HR professionals, for example, need to reframe challenges as opportunities for both the individual and the company to grow.

The problem I see is that practitioners in the HR profession are not purposeful or intentional in their communication on the HR objectives and how these add value to the business and how they add value to the people they serve.

This this indicates a lack of commitment to the intentional real HR value-adding areas, a lack of commitment to the base requirements and protocols of the profession and having the incorrect mindset.

It also may indicate a lack of understanding of the valuable role that HR plays in making the company successful.

Standards

The final foundational element centers on maintaining high professional standards when engaging with others and delivering HR services.

Standards matter for several reasons:

- **Consistency:** They ensure that all are evaluated and treated consistently. For example, a standardised performance review process helps in assessing all employees on the same criteria.

- **Clarity:** *They provide clear expectations for employees. Think of an employee handbook that outlines company policies on attendance, dress code, and disciplinary procedures.*

- **Compliance:** *They help in adhering to legal requirements, reducing the risk of non-compliance with labor laws and regulations."*

These standards serve as practical guidelines, ensuring tasks, processes, and interactions are handled efficiently, safely, and consistently. HR itself is built on foundational legislation that ensures fairness and equity in the workplace. Organisations enhance this framework by implementing policies, procedures, and codes of good practice, that are tailored to themselves, giving them a competitive edge. As a result, policies, such as parental leave, can differ between companies, with some offering more generous benefits than others.

The various Boards of Personnel Practitioners have also identified core strategic standards for the HR profession. Whilst these standards are essential, HR professionals must also uphold their own professional and personal standards. By doing so, they can build superior HR practice and elevate their impact within the field.

After each interaction between a professional, business leader and or employee, the critical question to reflect on is:

"How did I feel personally after that engagement with the professional or leader?" This evaluation helps assess whether the experience was positive, motivating, and aligned with your crown, core and contribution. Did they leave positive about their workplace and workspace, did they feel better about a situation, did they feel inspired and motivated on a challenge experienced, do they walk away seeing the challenge they presented as an opportunity to improve, enhance and do better. So, the practice of setting high and great personal engagement standards leads to great employee experience.

HR professionals in heightening and levelling up their awareness, conscious commitment, treatment of others and raising personal standards builds their personal capability further. Why is this important? Because we know that emotional intelligence in HR practices can enhance self-awareness and empathy, leading to better interpersonal relationships and better decision-making.

HR Professionals need to therefore have resilience so that they can bounce back, recover, or adapt successfully in the face of adversity, challenges, or significant sources of stress. It is the capacity to withstand, overcome, and even thrive during difficult circumstances that matters. **Being able to navigate these effectively and emerging stronger!** These are dynamic qualities that can be developed and strengthened over time. It plays a crucial role in personal well-being, mental health, and the capacity to navigate workplace challenges successfully whilst treating others with the necessary decorum. HR professionals and HR leaders must embrace the importance of awareness, commitment and intentional treatment of self and others with intentionality and the right mindset for greater results.

Placing the client at the center of HR efforts leads to:

- Faster buy-in for proposed HR interventions.

- Improved implementation efficiency and turnaround times.

- Enhanced employee engagement, experience, and customer satisfaction.

- Alignment with key HR strategic standards and core beliefs.

- Stronger commitment to fairness in addressing people-related matters.

This approach underscores the importance of mindset, guiding HR professionals in overcoming limiting beliefs and refining their practices.

HR Practice Notes provide a framework for both HR professionals and line managers, ensuring a strong foundation for success. By mastering Awareness, Conscious Commitment,

Fair Treatment, and Standards, HR professionals elevate their expertise and impact.

HR plays a crucial role in long-term business success by fostering transformation, team development, and a people-centered culture. Shifting from a task-based approach to one focused on awareness and well-being prevents costly setbacks while boosting retention, productivity, and talent attraction, ultimately strengthening company culture. Placing the client at the center of HR efforts leads to:

- Faster buy-in for proposed HR interventions.

- Improved implementation efficiency and turnaround times.

- Enhanced employee engagement, experience, and customer satisfaction.

- Alignment with key HR strategic standards and core beliefs.

- Stronger commitment to fairness in addressing people-related matters.

This approach underscores the importance of mindset, guiding HR professionals in overcoming limiting beliefs and refining their practices. HR Practice Notes provide a framework for both HR professionals and line managers, ensuring a strong foundation for success. By mastering Awareness, Conscious Commitment,

Fair Treatment, and Standards, HR professionals elevate their expertise and impact. HR plays a crucial role in long-term business success by fostering transformation, team development, and a people-centered culture. Shifting from a task-based approach to one focused on awareness and well-being prevents costly setbacks while boosting retention, productivity, and talent attraction, ultimately strengthening company culture.

HR professionals must be **equipped** to harness the human advantage by:

- Shifting employees from limiting beliefs to growth mindsets.

- Conducting capability assessments to boost confidence and team synergy.

- Receiving coaching for stronger commitment and follow-through.

- Learning and evaluating HR functional standards.

- Aligning personal values with the core principles of HR success.

By fostering awareness, commitment, and high standards, HR transcends its function to drive business success and growth. Through self-awareness, compassion, and continuous learning, HR professionals shape a workplace where individuals feel valued. By embracing emotional intelligence and setting inspiring standards, we create a culture of excellence.

Ultimately, HR needs to equip itself with the right mindset, awareness, commitment, and standards to ensure both employees and the organisation thrive together.

"We are the sum total of our experiences. Those experiences – be they positive or negative – make us the person we are, at any given point in our lives." – B.J. Neblett

Chapter Two

HR Strategic Journey for HR Impact and Success Through Activating a Great Employee Experience

As HR Professionals we have the power to serve well, all we need is to allow ourselves to claim it, share it and use it!

So, what do I mean by this?

This means that having the power to serve is akin to donning a superhero cape made from compassion, responsibility, and humility! This unique power equips HR professionals and leaders to act as everyday 'champions' in the workplace. Champions who are dedicated to making a positive impact on everyone's day at the office and the overall financial success of the business. It's about harnessing the strengths within to solve challenges, uplift colleagues, and create an environment where everyone can thrive.

By embracing this role, HR professionals become the catalysts for a brighter, more engaging, and supportive workplace. They use their keen understanding of human dynamics and their unwavering commitment to service to foster a culture of positivity, mutual respect and growth. They become the everyday heroes who transform ordinary workdays into extraordinary experiences.

Whether it's swooping in to solve workplace challenges or spreading smiles, it's all about using our powers for good and making the world a better place, one kind deed at a time, or as I said earlier one smiley face at a time.

> **6**
>
> **HR Professionals have the power to serve, so claim it, use it and share it.**

So, gear up and get ready to champion great employee engagement experiences one dynamic HR intervention and innovative solution at a time! Because at its core, the power to serve is about tuning into the needs of those around us, whether they are family, friends, or work colleagues. This is all about being a modern-day HR practice ready to adapt and flex within innovative solutions that fit like a perfectly tailored suit. So, let's get back to the core of what it means to be human and the true role of human resources, by adding meaningful improvements to every interaction. It's about delivering smiles and solutions in a simple, agile manner that truly highlights the human side of service.

The power to serve is about recognising the interconnectedness of our "humanness" and leveraging one's abilities and resources to make a positive impact within the world of work and the world. It is a mindset that prioritizes service and altruism, contributing to the greater good and fostering a sense of fulfillment and purpose in the workplace.

It's about using our unique talents and resources to sprinkle a little sunshine wherever we go, whether it's in the boardroom or at the local park. Think of it as having a superhero mindset, where every act of kindness is like a mini victory for the forces of good!

By embracing this spirit of service, we not only make our workplaces happier and healthier, but we also add a little extra sparkle to the world around us.

We must focus our efforts to **empower** our HR Professionals so that they are geared up to activate a great HR Practice that will enhance the experience in the workplace, by using our creativity and strategic insight to deliver impactful HR initiatives and interventions. By doing so, we can align our actions to drive greater commercial value and equity within the organisation. We must **empower** our HR professionals by showing them how to leverage people through innovative engagement practices, effective communication and cutting-edge technology to dramatically improve the employee experience. By combining expertise, creativity, and strategic insight, HR professionals can activate a high-performing HR practice that enhances both employee and business outcomes.

How we serve as HR Professionals is dependent on key factors that influence HR services, such as:

- Where are we operating institutionally based on the history and evolution of human resources.?
- How were we trained and developed within the profession in practice?
- Where our mindset is regarding our awareness, commitment, treatment of others and the standards we set.?

Let's embark on a journey through the evolution of HR, exploring how the naming of our HR practices have transformed over time. By understanding the historical shifts and advancements in HR, we can better appreciate the dynamic nature of this field and its critical role in shaping modern workplaces into the future. From its early days it focused on basic personnel management to its current strategic and holistic approach, the evolution of HR highlights the increasing importance of nurturing human capital to drive organisational success.

The Evolution of HR through Time:

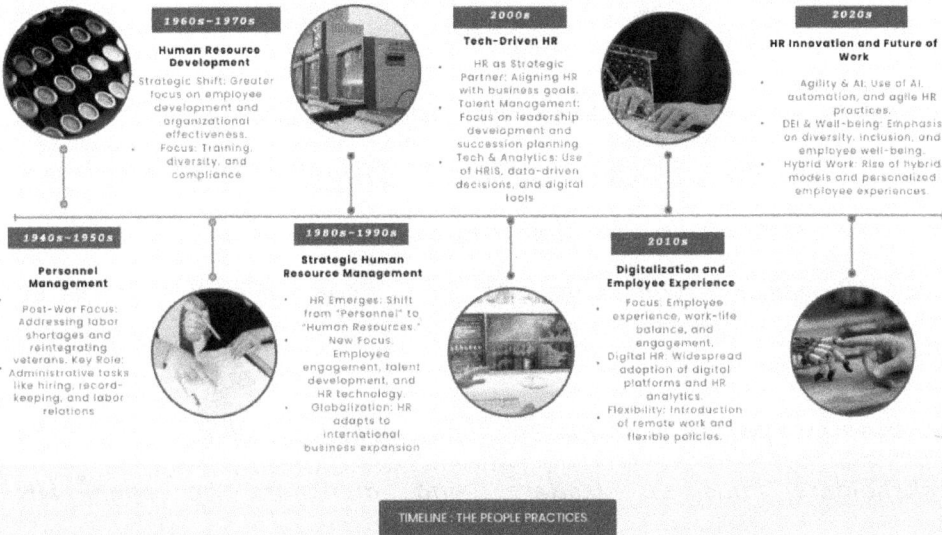

The History of HR

1960s–1970s
Human Resource Development
- Strategic Shift: Greater focus on employee development and organizational effectiveness.
- Focus: Training, diversity, and compliance

2000s
Tech-Driven HR
- HR as Strategic Partner: Aligning HR with business goals.
- Talent Management: Focus on leadership development and succession planning
- Tech & Analytics: Use of HRIS, data-driven decisions, and digital tools

2020s
HR Innovation and Future of Work
- Agility & AI: Use of AI, automation, and agile HR practices.
- DEI & Well-being: Emphasis on diversity, inclusion, and employee well-being.
- Hybrid Work: Rise of hybrid models and personalized employee experiences.

1940s–1950s
Personnel Management
- Post-War Focus: Addressing labor shortages and reintegrating veterans. Key Role: Administrative tasks like hiring, record-keeping, and labor relations

1980s–1990s
Strategic Human Resource Management
- HR Emerges: Shift from "Personnel" to "Human Resources." New Focus: Employee engagement, talent development, and HR technology.
- Globalization: HR adapts to international business expansion

2010s
Digitalization and Employee Experience
- Focus: Employee experience, work-life balance, and engagement.
- Digital HR: Widespread adoption of digital platforms and HR analytics.
- Flexibility: Introduction of remote work and flexible policies.

TIMELINE : THE PEOPLE PRACTICES

Through this timeline the function of HR has also evolved from Personnel to being Policy driven, to Partnering with Business, to being recognised as a Player alongside business, and now a Passion for People to drive individual and business growth albeit digitisation and what the future might hold in artificial intelligence. (AI). This I refer to as the **'P' trajectory** through time. i.e. from **Personnel, Policy, Partner, Player and to Passionate Advocate.**

HR personnel referred to the workforce of an organisation regardless of their specific roles or responsibilities and the traditional name given to an HR division. During this period, the profession was referred to as the personnel department where emphasis was placed on payroll activities and who worked in the organisation.

HR **policy** encompasses the rules and guidelines governing the various aspects of the workforce including the employer-employee relationship, so the traditional role played by HR was that of policing and throwing the book of rules back at employees.

HR business **partners** immerse themselves in collaborating with stakeholders, business leaders, and managers to align HR strategies and initiatives with the overall goals and business objectives of the company. HR partners serve as trusted advisors and consultants, providing strategic guidance and support to the business they serve. A Partner is an HR professional that connotes a sense of smoothness, confidence, and success in navigating relationships with business or their clients.

HR **players** actively participate in the execution and implementation of HR programmes, processes, and initiatives within an organisation. An HR Player knows and understands the business goals and objectives and fully understands when, through strategic alignment, how to identify the interventions and solutions for the business that would be of high impact and would make a difference to the organisation. HR players support businesses in the hands-on execution of business activities that are aligned with the key HR activities.

HR **passion advocates** reflect the enthusiasm and dedication of HR professionals to their work. It encompasses a genuine interest in supporting the organisation whilst advocating for employees, promoting a positive work culture, driving organisational change, and contributing to the commercial and financial success of the company through providing a superior best in class effective HR practice and a great employee experience.

The evolution of HR and how the HR professionals **position** themselves in relation to this trajectory is crucial as it determines how they provide a superior best-in-class HR offering that has an impact on the employee and the employer experience.

So, what I mean is that HR professionals who then play in or operate in the space as true players and show passion with energy on implementation win in providing a better experience as the focus is not only on the organisation but also on the person and how the intervention or solution would have an impact not only at the organisational level but also at the individual level.

Let's think about this more by exploring some of the critical challenges observed in the HR landscape. These hurdles not only hinder the efficiency of great HR practices but also present opportunities for significant transformation and innovation.

Some HR leaders and HR Professionals may not always be adequately geared up and or transformed to provide a superior HR practice or to serve employees in the company, as they are also sometimes only comfortable with using lengthy structured processes that are deemed traditional, as they have not kept up with the timeline as it relates to the evolution of HR. and or the business financial and performance cycle.

The result: they do not necessarily yield or provide results to the business that are relevant, timely, impactful with immediacy and to the employee at an individual level.

In some workplaces employee satisfaction or engagement levels are not where they should be due to poor employee experiences and the consequence of that is below-average engagement and working relations and or interpersonal relations between the staff and their leaders or even between HR professionals and line management.

7 *Activate your key value adding HR Services*	*Some HR Professionals do not know how to effectively implement an intervention at scale in the shortest time for greater impact. HR professionals often struggle with how to approach the business when it comes to implementing a value-adding*

intervention. Even more challenging is when they're unsure of the right solutions to propose. Without a clear strategy or understanding of what the business truly needs; it can feel overwhelming to present ideas that make a real impact.

Now here's the challenge I sometimes notice, HR Professionals may not always align their HR support interventions to the company's business financial performance cycle and outcomes in practice and this may lead to an overall poor engagement experience for the business leaders and the employees, ultimately resulting in poor business outcomes. And the consequence of this is that the business would experience a delay in achieving the results that they should have in the first instance due to the non -alignment and time delays. This may therefore indicate that HR Executives and professionals are not adequately geared up to serve by identifying the top strategic objectives for greatest engagement and impact within the business financial performance cycle with immediacy.

Some HR Professionals often do not activate their key value-adding practices to the business they serve with immediacy, which means they end up delaying the implementation of the strategic value-adding practices of HR and end up focusing on the HR functional areas only. This can result in unnecessary delays in the identification and implementation of best interventions, and because of the delay, the business would not see the expected results as quickly as they could like which means that human resources may not be adding value timeously.

This can result in negative consequences for HR, leading to a diminished great employee experience and a less-than-ideal client experience, which ultimately impacts the company's profits. Additionally, it can tarnish HR's reputation within the organisation, making it harder to build trust and drive positive change.

It's therefore very important for HR professionals to not only understand the key value-adding practices but to also know when and how to introduce these. So, to activate the delivery of a great superior HR Practice it must be understood that this level of service can be achieved through the activation of a great employee experience. As the HR functional areas are examples of HR Practices, we move off the premise that an HR professional knows and understands these.

So, the 5 key elements of goals, gameplan, guidance, gains and growth assist the HR professional to kickstart their HR practice in such a way that it immediately provides for a great employee experience. This can be done through the creation of an employee value proposition and the mapping of the employee life cycle and touchpoints.

As professionals, this gives you the confidence to quickly identify the key value-added HR practices that have a direct impact on the employee at each touchpoint and how these are the aligned to the strategic goals of the organisation.

At the core of these elements it means that the implementation of a superior HR Practice does not only begin with the HR strategy that is aligned to the business strategy, but it also considers the top 3-5 interventions of impact that will make a difference to both the employee and the business, considered through the goal setting process. This approach lays the foundation for HR professionals to create a happier, more engaged workforce and a positive workplace culture. From here, the HR strategic plan and roadmap are crafted collaboratively, guiding the organisation toward its goals with a clear, purpose-driven direction. Through this approach you can define the purpose and **Goals** of Human Resources.

This highlights the strategic value of an innovative game plan where both employees and the company benefit from an enhanced, uplifting employee experience. But beyond that, it's also about providing **guidance** and fostering **growth** for both individuals and the organisation.

Having purpose-driven goals with a strategic game plan that is aligned to the business strategic goals, allows HR professionals to have a greater impact on both employees and the company in a shorter space of time. HR goals need to be fully established at the outset and need to be aligned to the organisational goals.

Established purpose and goals are important as they solidify the 3-5 top strategic priorities that have been identified. What, however, remains important, is that the HR professionals need to extend the interventions that support these strategic goals to a great employee experience for greater HR impact and company results. This means that HR professionals need to become extremely creative in how they go about implementing the interventions or solutions as this demonstrates HR's value add to the people and the company.

HR professionals therefore need to advocate for better engagement with employees, through conversations and participation of their clients in the implementation of the HR strategic priorities at the individual level. This is a key goal that needs to appear in the strategic game plan.

HR practices play a crucial role in shaping the organisational culture and are essential for managing employees in a way that is passionate, inspiring, and uplifting, but does not fail to remain ahead of the curve by blending technology and AI into their future solutions.

Human Resources Value Proposition

HR professionals need to understand their company's strategic outlook, company culture in order to develop its unique value proposition for a far more enjoyable and greater employee and organisational experience.

> 8
>
> The Employee Value Proposition must prioritise people at its core.

When crafting your Employee Value Proposition (EVP), it's all about creating a clear and compelling messages that completely resonate with the people in the business. Your value proposition must prioritise people at its core.

By doing this, everyone will be able to:

- Understand the purpose behind the company's existence and the core values it stands for. Know the company culture and describe this through discussion and noting the key attributes that make it an attractive place to work.

- Identify and relate to the unique Employee Value Proposition (EVP) that sets the company apart from its competitors in the eyes of potential and current employees.

- Determine the key components of their EVP based on their organisation's culture, values, and the needs of their employees. This may include factors such as compensation, benefits, career development opportunities, work-life balance, company culture, and recognition.

- Gain deep insights into the needs, preferences, and motivations of the current employees and the future talent they want to retain and attract.

- Identify how the Employee Value Proposition (EVP) can support key business goals such as attracting top talent, reducing turnover, improving employee engagement, and driving company performance.

- Develop clear and compelling messaging that articulate the EVP to both internal and external audiences. Ensuring that the EVP messaging is consistent across all communication channels, including recruitment materials, job postings, employee handbooks, and internal communications.

- Measure the effectiveness of the EVP in attracting, retaining, and engaging employees. It's crucial to regularly evaluate your EVP and adjust as needed based on feedback from employees and changes in the external environment.

- Regularly conduct surveys, interviews, and focus groups to understand what matters most to the leadership and employees in their work environment and employment experience, to foster employee engagement and loyalty, which drives business success.

Once an HR professional fully understands all the above fundamental messages, the HR Strategy can be formulated in alignment with the company's strategic outlook. And financial performance cycle.

The foundational strategic elements that will be contained within the HR strategy include the attraction, development and retention of valuable employees. So, for example, if your HR vision is to:

"Be an Employer of Choice" and the HR Mission is: "The Best People Drive Our Business "or "We Create Journeys to Enrich Our Employee Experience".

The **HR Strategic Objectives** are to:

- "Attract and identify the right talent "
- "Develop and grow the right skills and competencies, to create a high-performance culture for greater competitive advantage"

- "Retain and reward higher performing employees by enhancing employee engagement and experience to create a culture of innovation learning and fun".
- "Deploy key employees into critical business areas for skills and knowledge transfer to build company future capacity and capability
- "Build effective leadership teams that develop future leadership capability"

To achieve this, it's essential that HR professionals deliver on promises made to their employees as this is central to providing a great employee experience. This means providing the benefits, rewards, and opportunities that you have promised and by continuously seeking feedback to ensure that your EVP remains relevant and impactful, as the employee life cycle remains dynamic as it should be ever evolving and agile to maintain great employee experiences.

The Employee Life Cycle:

Employee Life Cycle & Touchpoints

The Eight Key Stages of an Employee's Journey

Touchpoint 5

8: Rehiring and Offboarding

Managing exits through resignations, retirements, or terminations, while maintaining positive relationships.

1: Seek Talent

How the company draws attention from potential candidates through employer branding, advertising, and referrals.

Touchpoint 1

7: Performance and Progression

Monitoring and evaluating employees' work contributions and aligning them with organizational goals. Offering promotions, career pathing, or lateral moves to help employees advance within the organization.

2: Recruit Talent

The active process of seeking, interviewing, and selecting the right candidates for open roles.

Touchpoint 4

6: Talent and Retention

Strategies aimed at keeping top talent engaged and satisfied within the organization.

3: Pre-board & Outboard

The introduction and integration of new hires into the company culture, ensuring a smooth start

Touchpoint 3

5: Training and Development

Opportunities for professional growth and skill enhancement through training, mentoring, and workshops

4: Employee Engagement

Investment in Human Capital as a strategic advantage to elevate the companies performance and competitive edge in the market

Touchpoint 2

The Employee Life Cycle has several stages, starting with recruitment and concludes when an employee completes the offboarding process. This is the journey that the employee undertakes as they enter the company up until such time they leave or exit the company.

It's important to understand that from recruitment to offboarding there are intermediary stages. The stages are distinguished based on the employee life cycle and take note that the number of stages may vary depending on the company and its operating model. Within the employee life cycle stages some of the stages may be an ongoing activity. Within the employee lifecycle, there are various touchpoints that HR professionals can leverage to enhance the employee experience.

Mastering the Employee Life Cycle stages through their effective implementation by HR Professionals is essential for a great employee experience, as the employee life cycle is linked to this.

So, HR professionals need to engage with each stage to better understand the needs of the employee and how their employee experience including their own experience can be enhanced and improved at each stage.

Stage 1: Seek Talent

To truly elevate the employee experience of the HR professional during this critical stage. This stage corresponds with all the talent attraction activities. So, your organisation will be searching for talent, researching candidates and checking resumes and application letters. Whilst at this stage, networking events or career events can provide good opportunities for seeking talent. Many employees participate in referral programmes, thus benefiting from recommendations from friends or family to facilitate access to the recruitment stage.

Leveraging advanced technologies such as AI-driven recruitment platforms can significantly enhance candidate sourcing and screening, ensuring that you identify the best fit for your organisation swiftly and efficiently. Engaging with potential candidates through various digital channels, including social media and professional networks, can broaden your reach and attract top-tier talent. Moreover, creating a robust employer brand that highlights your organisation's unique culture and values will make your company more appealing to prospective employees.

Additionally, fostering strong relationships with educational institutions and industry associations can create a pipeline of skilled candidates. Hosting or participating in webinars and virtual career fairs can also provide valuable touchpoints with talent, especially in today's increasingly remote work environment. By blending new, innovative HR strategies (such as AI-driven recruitment, employer branding, and personalized employee experiences) with proven traditional methods (like structured interviews, referrals, and career development programs), HR professionals can build a well-rounded talent attraction strategy. This approach not only improves the HR professional's effectiveness, making their job easier and more impactful, but also helps the organisation attract and retain top talent by offering a competitive and engaging employee experience.

Stage 2: Recruit Talent

Enhancing the experience of line management is crucial during the recruitment stage. Even though organisations use various methods and activities during the recruitment phase, the goal remains the same, which is to recruit and onboard the best candidates. By equipping line managers with advanced recruitment tools, effective training programs, and clear communication channels, they can more efficiently identify and engage top talent. This not only streamlines the hiring process but also ensures that new hires are well-aligned with the organisation's goals and culture, setting the stage for long-term success and growth.

The prospective employee will usually be invited to this stage of the employee life cycle, so herein lies the opportunity for a great memorable experience, such that the prospect looks forward to joining the company. An interview is the most classic recruitment activity that most employees must go through before gaining employment in a company. There are several ways to carry out the interviews depending on the scope and focus, as well as the overall structure of the recruitment cycle.

Here are a few examples of the modern-day interviewing processes:

- Traditional In-Person Interviews: Face-to-face interviews are conducted at the workplace or a neutral location.
- Phone Interviews: Initial screening interviews are conducted over the phone to assess basic qualifications and interests.
- Video Interviews: Interviews are conducted via video conferencing platforms like Zoom, Skype, or Microsoft Teams.
- Panel Interviews: Interviews where multiple interviewers from different departments or roles ask questions in a single session.
- Group Interviews: Interviews where multiple candidates are interviewed together to observe interactions and assess teamwork skills.
- Technical Interviews: Specialised interviews focusing on specific technical skills or problem-solving abilities, often including practical tasks or coding tests.
- Behavioural Interviews: Interviews that focus on past behaviour and experiences to predict future performance,

often using the STAR method (Situation, Task, Action, Result).

- Case Interviews: Interviews where candidates are given a business problem to solve, commonly used in consulting and management roles.

- Assessment Centres: A series of exercises, including group discussions, presentations, and role-playing, conducted over one or more days to evaluate multiple competencies.

- Structured Interviews: Interviews with a standardised set of questions asked to all candidates to ensure consistency and fairness.

- Unstructured Interviews: More informal interviews with open-ended questions, allowing for a more conversational and flexible approach.

- Competency-Based Interviews: Interviews focused on assessing specific competencies or skills relevant to the job role.

- Remote Interviews: Interviews are conducted entirely online, allowing candidates to participate from any location, often used for remote or hybrid roles.

- AI-Powered Interviews: Automated interviews conducted by AI software that analyses responses and assesses candidates based on predefined criteria.

Obviously, the type of role and the level of seniority will influence the structure and number of phases of recruitment.

For example, a mid-seniority Finance professional might first be invited to a non-technical interview conducted by the HR manager/recruiter. The purpose will be to cross check the resume and experience the level of the candidate as well as provide the candidate with information regarding the role and the overall organisation. Once this step is successfully completed, the candidate might be invited to participate in a technical test case. Here the goal is to ensure that they possess the required technical skills and knowledge required to do the job. A successful conclusion to the recruitment stage is signing a new employment contract. The contract will provide key information regarding the start date, the working hours and location, compensation, duties and obligations, and so on.

Point to Ponder? Take a moment to reflect on your current interview process. Could it be enhanced by incorporating more modern and innovative approaches?

Stage 3: Pre-boarding and Onboarding Experience

The prospective employees experience needs to be enhanced, so it's important to provide a pre and onboarding experience that is engaging. Once the new employees sign the contract, the pre- & onboarding processes begin. The preboarding process offers the prospective employee an opportunity to familiarise themselves with the company and it also allows them to start building a relationship with their new team, line manager and overall organisation. The onboarding process is inclusive of the first day on the job and has two main purposes: cultural-social integration and relationship-building as well as the provision of all the information and skills necessary to become a productive member of the team. Pre & onboarding processes are there to properly integrate a new hire into a company. When you integrate a new hire successfully into a new company, they will be engaged, productive, perform well and feel satisfied with their job.

Stage 4: Employee Engagement

It's important that you at this stage boost your employee's engagement for a better experience. The talent and the skills of employees will be the distinguishing factor. They will explain why an organisation's business, product or service is better than the rest of the competition. The longer the employment relationship and the employee lifecycle, the more valuable of an asset you become for your company. As highlighted by management consulting firm Korn Ferry, organizations with highly engaged employees can generate 2.5 times more revenue compared to those with low engagement. It's clear that when employees are invested and motivated, the positive impact on a company's bottom line is significant. Therefore, companies need to implement strategies and practices that promote engagement, support career growth, and ensure employees feel valued and motivated. This investment in human capital is not just a benefit to the employees but a strategic advantage that can significantly elevate the company's performance and competitive edge in the market.

Stage 5: Provide Training through Development

The employee's development needs to be encouraged through their training for an enhanced experience. Career development is a crucial factor that influences employees' decisions to accept a job or stay with a company. Generally speaking, no one wants to feel stuck in a job doing the same thing with no prospect of improvement and career advancement.

Development is achievable through participating in training courses and taking advantage of upskilling opportunities. When employees feel like they have room for growth and development, they are more prone to feel engaged with their employer. This leads to longer employment relationships and significantly improves your company's retention rate.

Stage 6: Talent Retention

To sustain a productive and dedicated workforce, it is crucial to focus on talent retention. This involves implementing a variety of strategies aimed at keeping employees motivated and satisfied with their roles in the organisation. By creating a positive work environment where employees feel valued, offering competitive benefits, and providing opportunities for career progression, companies can retain top talent and reduce turnover rates. Regularly recognising and rewarding employees for their contributions can also foster a sense of belonging and loyalty to the company. These instruments create a framework for gaining a better overview of their journey through the company. Additionally, employees can provide inputs into how the workplace could better accommodate their needs and desires.

Stage 7: Performance and Progression

Monitoring and evaluating employees work contributions and aligning them with organisational goals remains paramount. Offering promotions, career pathing, or lateral moves to help employees advance within the organisation is important.

Stage 8: Offboarding and Rehiring

It's important that you prepare for a good offboarding process to enhance the employee experience as they become the alumni who promote the company and the remarkable things that it does for its staff of the company, as alumni after they have left the company. So regardless of the type of termination that is whether it is voluntary or not, offboarding comprises the final activities leading up to the employees' exit from the company. There will be many administrative activities to ensure the closure of the contract. For example, handover of equipment, final reporting on tasks and progress made in the job and eventual training of the replacement for the role. But offboarding is more than administrative work. When done right, offboarding processes ensure a cordial relationship between themselves and their now former employer. During Rehiring there are times when this can happen, especially during leaves of absence, which don't quite fit neatly into the typical employee life cycle. For instance, employees might go through a reboarding process after returning from maternity leave or an extended sick leave, helping them ease back into their roles smoothly. This stage is not a mandatory stage in the life cycle of the employee; however, we mention it as employees who leave and return for varying reasons would have had an offboarding experience. In summary, rehiring may occur under specific circumstances, such as after a leave of absence, maternity leave, or long sick leave, although it is not a mandatory stage in the employee's life cycle. It is important to consider as it involves employees who have previously undergone an offboarding experience and are now returning to the organisation.

The Employee Touch Points

Here are the key touch-points along with strategies for HR professionals to enhance the employee experience.

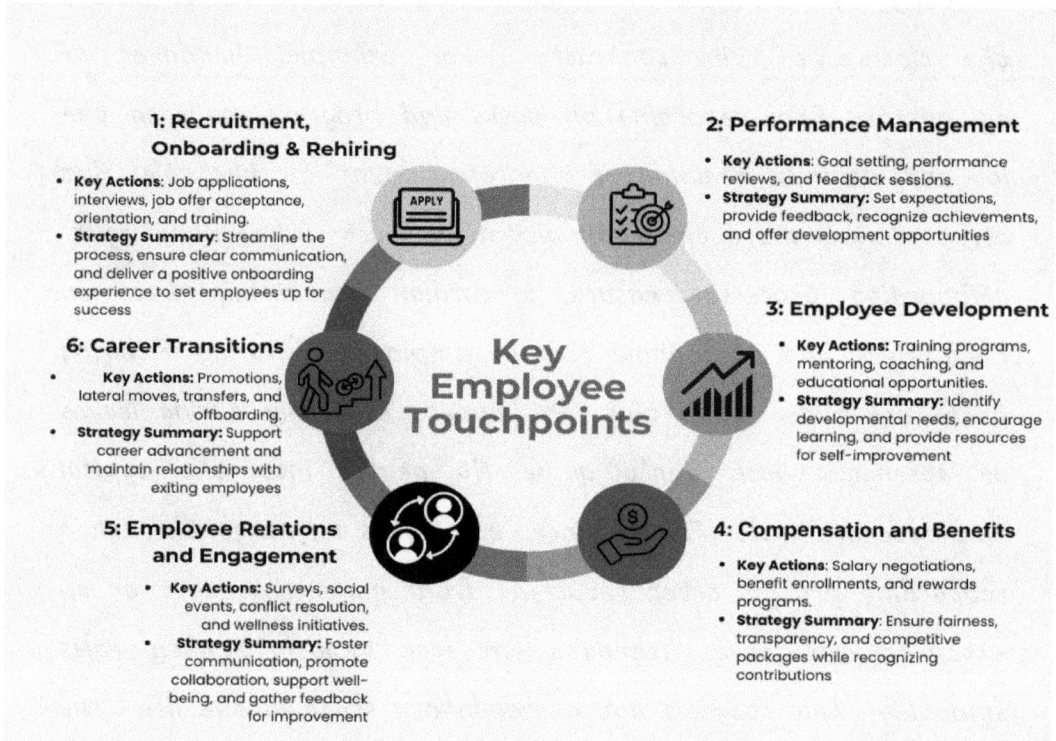

1: Recruitment, Onboarding & Rehiring
- **Key Actions**: Job applications, interviews, job offer acceptance, orientation, and training.
- **Strategy Summary**: Streamline the process, ensure clear communication, and deliver a positive onboarding experience to set employees up for success

2: Performance Management
- **Key Actions**: Goal setting, performance reviews, and feedback sessions.
- **Strategy Summary**: Set expectations, provide feedback, recognize achievements, and offer development opportunities

3: Employee Development
- **Key Actions**: Training programs, mentoring, coaching, and educational opportunities.
- **Strategy Summary**: Identify developmental needs, encourage learning, and provide resources for self-improvement

4: Compensation and Benefits
- **Key Actions**: Salary negotiations, benefit enrollments, and rewards programs.
- **Strategy Summary**: Ensure fairness, transparency, and competitive packages while recognizing contributions

5: Employee Relations and Engagement
- **Key Actions**: Surveys, social events, conflict resolution, and wellness initiatives.
- **Strategy Summary**: Foster communication, promote collaboration, support well-being, and gather feedback for improvement

6: Career Transitions
- **Key Actions**: Promotions, lateral moves, transfers, and offboarding.
- **Strategy Summary**: Support career advancement and maintain relationships with exiting employees

Key Employee Touchpoints

A crucial part of the strategy is ensuring support at key transition points. This includes providing career advancement and mobility opportunities, assisting employees as they move into new roles or departments, conducting exit interviews to understand departure reasons, and maintaining positive relationships with former employees for potential rehiring or referrals.

By focusing on each touch-point throughout the employee lifecycle, HR professionals can create a positive employee experience that enhances engagement, retention, and overall organisational success. Its for this reason that HR Executives and HR Professionals need to be geared up and adequately resourced to support and undertake theses responsibilities.

HR professionals can measure their success by incorporating comprehensive employee engagement surveys that address effective HR practices. These surveys should be designed to gather continuous feedback for ongoing improvement in HR functions. HR professionals can then be guided on how to leverage and shape their HR purpose and goals. Then together create a strategic HR roadmap that aligns with the organisation's broader objectives. To maximise value, we show you how to customise key organisational touch-points by identifying and referencing to areas of HR value, and how to effectively implement tailored HR solutions based on the identified areas.

This enhancement of HR practice comes to life when HR professionals understand the history of HR and recognise their position within this evolving trajectory. Through facilitated discussions, the HR team evaluates where they stand in relation to these historical benchmarks. Additionally, employee and client feedback from engagement surveys provides valuable insights into their experience of a great HR practice.

The added benefit is that HR will be **empowered** to not only facilitate the development of their own strategic roadmap and game plan but will be able to better support the line through a similar facilitation process for the company. All interventions that arise out of the collaboration will therefore result in a shared understanding of what needs to be undertaken, and the business would also drive the placement of the required resources for the implementation of the identified interventions.

9

A superior HR Practice contributes to the overall productive management of human capital within the organisation

10

In Practice leadership needs to be trained on the people elements that need focus

In summary, the activation begins with the employee HR process, focusing on the swift and effective execution of HR interventions. So, Establishing and providing a superior HR Practice contributes to the overall productive management of human capital within an organisation, so that HR Professionals support business in practice from the onset.

HR professionals are also empowered to have conversations with the business on the areas that have an impact on the employee touch points and what is expected of their clients in each of these areas to improve their people practices and to enhance the experience of their direct reports.

It, therefore, begins with investing in and developing strong leaders at all levels of the organisation. To leverage human capital potential leadership needs to be trained in practice on the people elements that need focus. This includes leaders hiring individuals with diverse skill sets experiences and perspectives to enrich the organisation.

Leaders and HR need to make sure that all employees feel valued, respected, and supported and this can only be possible when an inclusive environment is created, as diversity would be embraced, and it creates a culture of belonging where everyone can thrive.

To foster creativity, problem solving and a sense of belonging amongst people, collaboration and teamwork is to be encouraged across functions and divisions. People need to understand the company's vision, and goals, and how their individual contributions contribute to the larger picture. To achieve this communication channels, need to be open and transparent at all levels of the organisation. Empowered employees are more likely to be engaged, curious, innovative, and committed to achieving organisational goals. They take initiative, drive positive change, and contribute to a dynamic and thriving workplace culture.

Provide employees with autonomy to make decisions and take ownership of their work empowers them way beyond many other incentives. Due to the nature of work today it's important to promote a healthy work-life balance to prevent burnout and maintain employee well-being and this can be inclusive of flexible working arrangements, wellness programs and policies that support employees personal and family needs.

Recognise and reward employees for their achievements and contributions and this can be done through monetary incentives and non -monetary rewards such as praise and appreciation programs, promotions and or additional responsibilities.

> **11**
>
> **HR to institutionalise business support and collaboration by showing up in all these areas!**

Investing in the learning and development of employees to enhance their skills knowledge and abilities can be done in a formal and an informal mentorship opportunity. Implement performance management that provides regular feedback coaching and opportunities for growth for both the individual and the company. This helps employees to understand their strengths and improve their performance which is aligned to the organisational objectives. Human Resources leadership and professionals must institutionalise business support and collaboration by showing up in all these areas!

In summary, the phrase means that HR should actively establish and integrate itself into various aspects of the business by being present and involved in different areas. The goal is to ensure that HR is playing a key role in supporting and fostering collaboration across the organisation. By "showing up" in these areas, HR can build stronger relationships, provide necessary support, and help create a more cohesive and effective work environment.

How can the above be effectively implemented in practice?

By referencing practical examples within the touchpoints, HR professionals can access a quick point of reference for proven interventions that have been successfully executed.

For instance, during the recruitment touchpoint, using structured interviews and candidate assessment tools can streamline the hiring process and ensure the selection of top talent. In the onboarding phase, a well-designed orientation programme and mentorship initiative can significantly improve new employee integration.

Regular performance reviews and feedback sessions during the development touchpoint can help in identifying skill gaps and providing targeted training. Effective use of employee surveys and engagement platforms in the retention touchpoint can foster a positive work environment and address any concerns promptly.

These practical examples not only provide peace of mind but also elevate the strategic approach of HR professionals, ensuring they have a solid game plan to enhance their HR practices. HR professionals would have a quick point of reference on proven interventions that have been implemented and worked thus giving them peace of mind and levelling them up in terms of their game plan.

In addition to the above points, consideration should be given to startup and existing organisations.

Activating a superior best-in-class HR practice through great employee experiences is essential, whether your business is in its early stages or well-established. The second dimension of creating these top-tier HR practices is centred around elevating the employee experience by focusing on strategic, thoughtful practices that foster engagement, growth, and alignment with company goals.

So, whether your business is just starting up or already established, creating a great human resource practice is essential for ensuring a positive employee experience and fostering a thriving work environment. For HR professionals, the focus should be on setting clear goals and having a well-thought-out game plan that is aligned to the company goals that supports the growth of both the people and the leadership within the company. This also needs to be linked to your employee value proposition.

When your business is in the startup phase, laying a strong HR foundation is crucial. Start with clear, transparent goals that align with the company's mission and values. As an HR professional, your role is to create a game plan that attracts top talent while building a culture that fosters belonging and growth from day one. Focus on developing a structured onboarding process to guide new hires and give them a clear understanding of their role and how they can contribute to the company's success.

In a startup environment, where roles can be more fluid and employees often wear multiple hats, it's equally important to provide opportunities for growth. Mentorship programs, regular feedback sessions, and clear avenues for professional development allow employees to see a path for their growth within the company. Startups have the advantage of being nimble and dynamic, which provides the perfect environment for continuous learning and skill development. When employees feel they are growing both personally and professionally, they are more engaged and motivated to contribute to the company's success.

For startups, the goal is to build a solid HR foundation that will set the tone for the company culture and employee experience. When your business is just getting off the ground, the key is to set clear, transparent goals that align with your company's mission and values. HR professionals play a crucial role in ensuring that these values are communicated effectively and that they permeate the company culture from the beginning.

Equally important is ensuring opportunities for growth. Startups can offer a dynamic environment where employees can wear many hats, but it's vital to provide continuous learning and development. This can be made possible through mentorship, setting up regular feedback sessions, and ensuring that employees have a path for growth, both personally and professionally. This attention to employee experience will not only retain talent but also inspire greater contributions from your team.

For established businesses, the focus shifts from building foundational systems to refining and evolving existing HR practices. Here, the challenge is to ensure that HR systems continue to align with the company's long-term vision while meeting the evolving needs of both employees and leadership.

A key aspect of maintaining a great employee experience in established companies is refining goals to ensure they stay relevant. Leadership must be actively involved in setting these goals and modelling behaviour that reflects the company's values. When leadership demonstrates a commitment to the company's culture and employee well-being, it sets the tone for the rest of the organisation.

In addition, continuous growth and guidance are essential to keeping employees engaged in established businesses. Offering leadership development programs, clear career paths, and regular performance reviews help employees understand how they can progress within the organization. By fostering a culture of continuous feedback, HR can ensure that employees feel heard and supported in their roles. This not only strengthens employee loyalty but also empowers them to take ownership of their growth.

Investing in training and development programs is equally important in an established business. As companies grow, so do the expectations of their employees. Providing opportunities for skill development and growth not only improves individual performance but also reinforces the company's commitment to its workforce. A company that invests in its employees' development is one that attracts top talent and retains high-performing individuals.

In both cases, whether a startup or an established business, the key to great HR practices is in providing a clear path for gain, guidance and growth. By focusing on the holistic development of both employees and leadership, HR professionals play a vital role in ensuring the success of the company through a motivated, engaged, and empowered workforce.

Having good HR practices isn't just about creating a pleasant workplace, it's also a smart financial move for any company. Let me share two examples to show how effective HR can positively impact the bottom line.

First off, let's talk about employee retention. When HR professionals set clear goals and provide a solid game plan for employees' gain, guidance, and growth, people feel valued and see a future with the company. This leads to higher job satisfaction and lowers the chances of employees jumping ship. Now, why does this matter financially? Employee turnover is expensive. Recruiting, hiring, and training new staff not only costs money but also takes time. By keeping your talented team members on board, you save on these costs and maintain productivity levels, which is a direct financial benefit.

Secondly, effective HR practices boost overall productivity. When employees are guided and have opportunities to grow, they're more engaged and motivated to contribute their best work. This heightened productivity means projects get completed more efficiently, and the quality of work improves. For the company, this can lead to increased revenues, whether through the ability to take on more clients, improve customer satisfaction, or innovate new products and services. Essentially, an engaged workforce driven by strong HR leadership translates into better financial performance. For example, Google has long emphasised employee engagement through various initiatives like continuous learning, health benefits, and creating an innovative work environment.

The Employee Engagement and Turnover Cost is a usual HR-related metric that companies use. Companies may explicitly mention costs related to turnover, recruitment, and training in their financial statements. For instance, they might quantify the cost savings achieved through reduced turnover rates or improved employee engagement initiatives. So, investing in good HR practices pays off. It's all about nurturing your people so they can contribute more effectively to the company's success, which in turn leads to tangible financial gains.

On the other hand, the financial implications of an HR professional not having good practices can be significant, affecting both the short-term and long-term success of a business. Poor HR practices can lead to high employee turnover, disengagement, and even legal issues, all of which can drain a company's resources and hinder its growth. When HR professionals fail to create a positive and supportive environment, the ripple effect can be costly in more ways than one. For example, let's consider the cost of high employee turnover. When HR does not provide a strong foundation for employee engagement, professional growth, and well-being, employees are more likely to leave. The financial cost of replacing a single employee can be substantial, often ranging from 50% to 200% of that employee's annual salary. Source Gallup: https://www.gallup.com/workplace/247391/fixable-problem-costs-businesses-trillion.aspx).

This includes expenses related to recruitment, training, and the time it takes for new hires to become fully productive. Additionally, high turnover impacts team morale and productivity, causing further financial strain as the remaining employees may become overworked or disengaged. Another example is the legal risks that come with poor HR practices. If HR professionals do not ensure compliance with labour laws or fail to address employee concerns such as harassment or discrimination, the company can face lawsuits or regulatory fines.

These legal issues not only result in significant legal fees and potential settlements, but they also damage the company's reputation. The financial burden from such cases can be devastating, particularly for smaller companies, and can easily be avoided with good HR practices that emphasize proper communication, conflict resolution, and adherence to workplace laws. The lack of sound HR practices can severely impact a company's bottom line. Investing in strong HR strategies isn't just about compliance or keeping employees happy, it's about protecting the company's financial health by fostering a productive, loyal workforce and minimizing avoidable risks. Mastering the activation of a superior HR practice, is essential for driving immediate and long-term business success. Strong HR practices lead to lower turnover, increased engagement, and higher productivity, all of which have direct financial benefits. On the flip side, neglecting good HR practices can result in costly turnover, decreased morale, and even legal risks. Ultimately, investing in people and their growth isn't just about creating a better workplace, it's a smart HR Strategy that considers the financial people aspects that drives sustainable success for the business.

Whether you are just starting or refining existing practices, it's important to view HR as a strategic partner in business success. The role of HR goes beyond managing day-to-day operations; it's about fostering a thriving work environment where employees feel valued, supported, and empowered to contribute to the company's vision. This approach ensures that the organisation is not just retaining talent but also creating a culture where both people and the business can flourish.

Therefore, elevating the employee experience through great HR practices, whether in a startup or an established company, requires a clear vision, structured growth opportunities, and a commitment to aligning individual and organizational goals. By doing so, HR professionals help build a thriving workforce that drives long-term success for the company.

Here are some examples of case studies and statistics that highlight the impact of effective HR practice implementation, leading to improved employee engagement, retention, productivity, and overall company performance:

- Employee Engagement & Retention: Google's employee-centric policies contribute to high retention rates, aligning with research showing that engaged teams boost profitability by 21%.
- Productivity & Performance: Southwest Airlines fosters a strong culture, leading to higher productivity. Studies show happy employees are 12% more productive.

- *Talent Development: LinkedIn's focus on upskilling helps attract and retain top talent, with 94% of employees staying longer when companies invest in career growth.*
- *Diversity & Inclusion: IBM's inclusive hiring and training programs enhance innovation, with diverse teams being 36% more likely to achieve above-average profitability.*
- *Cost Containment: Costco's investment in employee compensation results in higher productivity, loyalty, and lower turnover, proving that strong HR practices improve financial performance.*

These case studies demonstrate the measurable impact of strategic HR interventions on business success. Several HR trends were gaining traction and shaping the way organisations approach talent management, employee engagement, and workplace culture. Here are some of the latest HR trends that may continue to evolve and influence the field:

So, while HR trends may come and go, the heart of HR remains the same: creating a workplace where people feel valued, supported, and ready to bring their best selves to the workplace every day.

Here are some key trends Shaping the Future, and that can activate **a great employee experience:**

- *Remote & Hybrid Work: Flexible work models are here to stay, requiring HR to refine virtual collaboration, remote policies, and employee well-being strategies.*

- *Employee Well-being & Mental Health: Organisations are prioritising mental health support, work-life balance, and stress reduction initiatives.*

- *Diversity, Equity & Inclusion (DEI): Companies are investing in diversity training, inclusive hiring, and accountability measures to foster belonging.*

- *Data-Driven HR: Predictive analytics and AI tools are transforming HR decision-making in recruitment, performance management, and workforce planning.*

- *Agile HR: Flexible, iterative approaches to goal setting and talent development help organizations adapt to change more efficiently.*

- *Continuous Learning: Upskilling and reskilling programs are key to employee growth and long-term career development.*

- *Remote Employee Engagement: Digital tools, virtual team building, and recognition programs keep employees connected and motivated.*

- *HR Technology & Automation: AI-powered recruitment, chatbots, and HRIS platforms streamline operations and enhance employee experiences.*

- Flexible Benefits & Total Rewards: Personalized benefits, wellness programs, and financial assistance options cater to evolving employee needs.
- Sustainability & CSR: HR is integrating corporate social responsibility initiatives, aligning workplace policies with environmental and social impact goals.

HR is evolving rapidly, blending technology, strategy, and employee-centric practices to build a more dynamic and inclusive workplace. Elevating the employee experience through effective HR practices is not only about fostering a positive workplace but also a smart financial strategy that impacts a company's bottom line. According to Gallup here's why:

- Employee Retention & Financial Impact: Effective HR strategies reduce costly turnover by providing clear goals, growth opportunities, and support, leading to a stable and motivated workforce.
- Productivity & Engagement: Engaged employees are up to 21% more productive, with HR-driven development, learning, and recognition boosting motivation and business growth.
- Cost of Poor HR Practices: Weak HR strategies contribute to high turnover, legal risks, and disengagement, costing U.S. businesses up to $1 trillion annually.

- *Long-term Value Creation:* Data-driven HR practices and continuous learning foster innovation, keeping businesses competitive and ensuring sustainable success.

In short, investing in superior HR practices not only boosts employee retention and productivity but also helps avoid costly mistakes, builds a positive company culture, and drives long-term business growth. The business impacts of HR investments have been seen by companies like Google and it's for this reason that they prioritise HR initiatives, such as health benefits, workplace innovation, and professional development, to boost engagement, productivity, and retention.

High turnover costs (50-200% of an employee's salary) highlights the need for strategic HR practices. By investing in employee well-being, recognition programs, and career growth, businesses reduce turnover, enhance workplace stability, and achieve long-term financial gains. These upfront investments improve company culture and directly contribute to profitability.

So, in conclusion the HR strategic journey is centered on harnessing the power to serve, creating exceptional employee experiences, and continuously enhancing HR practices. HR professionals play a crucial role in shaping a culture of empathy, responsibility, and growth, directly impacting both employee satisfaction and company success. By activating a great employee experience, HR professionals can design strategies that align employee engagement with business goals, ensuring employees feel valued, supported, and motivated. This involves optimizing the employee lifecycle from onboarding to career growth while leveraging modern technology to enhance efficiency. HR has evolved from traditional personnel management into a strategic function that drives business performance. Understanding key elements such as the Employee Value Proposition (EVP), critical employee life cycle touchpoints, and targeted interventions allows HR professionals to focus on high-impact areas that directly contribute to company success. Tools like employee engagement surveys, strategic activators and HR practice notes can provide measurable ways to refine HR practices and create a best-in-class experience.

Essential Actions to **enable** HR Leaders and Professionals more:

- Identify and focus on HR strategies that deliver real business value.
- Set clear HR goals aligned with organisational objectives.
- Use a purpose-driven approach to communicate and execute HR strategies.

- Develop resilience and adaptability to handle the complexities of the HR role.
- Define 3-5 critical areas of impact that drive company performance and profitability.
- Craft a compelling Employee Value Proposition (EVP) to showcase HR's contribution to business success.
- Prioritise the HR areas of investment for a great return.

Points to Ponder:

o What do HR Professionals need to do to support business in practice from the onset?

o How can the above be effectively implemented in practice?

Superior HR practice is not just about fostering a great workplace, it's a key driver of financial success. By strategically enhancing employee retention, boosting productivity, and reducing risks, HR professionals play a crucial part in creating a culture that has tangible financial benefit outcomes for their organisations. Ultimately, HR needs to **empower** its practices to ensure that both employees and the organisation thrive together.

"If you don't drive your business, you will be driven out of business." B.C. Forbes

Chapter Three

Creating a Consistent Image of Growth

Through the People to Profit Pathway

A great human and employee experience should be accessible to everyone, as it centres around connection, collaboration, and teamwork, ensuring that people feel they belong and can contribute value to the company. To achieve this, it's crucial for HR professionals to master the art of positioning HR effectively and accurately. This involves positioning HR through an employee value proposition that fosters a positive employee experience, creating a consistent image and narrative of growth for both the employee and the company. HR Professionals also need to position great engagement practices in terms of their value add and impact to the company's bottom line, through the people to profit pathway.

This will make people including HR professionals have a sense of belonging and they will feel empowered to contribute meaningfully to the company's success. Creating an environment where people feel they truly belong starts with fostering strong connections and a sense of commitment. This can be achieved by having an:

- Inclusive Culture: through valuing diversity and acceptance

- Strong Relationships: Creating opportunities for building connections with colleagues.

- Supportive Leadership: Empathetic leaders who listen and mentor for results.

- Shared Values: Alignment with the organization's mission.

- Recognition: Acknowledgment of contributions.

- Open Communication: through transparency and feedback.

- Growth Opportunities: Creating clear pathways for professional development.

- Recognition for performance and contribution to company success and the bottom line

In this context, all these factors are crucial in championing the implementation of great employee experiences. Too often, I observe HR professionals working behind the scenes, outshined by the company, instead of positioning HR in a way that highlights its direct contribution to the company's bottom line. It's vital for HR to step into the spotlight and demonstrate its value in driving both employee success and organisational growth.

Creating a work environment where individuals not only feel they belong but also feel truly valued is essential. It's about recognising and embracing the true character and nature of each person. After all, it's the people who drive success and innovation in any organisation. This is why it's crucial to ensure that the right people are in the right roles and that HR plays an active role in **positioning** human resources to direct a happier, more productive workplace.

As HR professionals, **enabling** others is just as important as having self-awareness. It's vital to truly understand your employees by getting to understand what they value, what motivates them, and what they aspire to achieve. When individuals feel a sense of belonging and the ability to contribute meaningfully, their engagement and commitment grow. These insights become the anchors that keep both professionals, and the broader team aligned with the company's goals. This alignment not only strengthens internal culture but also enhances the customer experience, positioning the company for expanded market reach and sustained growth.

The key to success lies in empowering HR and leadership to craft memorable engagement experiences in the workplace. So, Make Moments Matter!

When people feel enabled, empowered and connected, they can contribute to building a culture of growth, innovation, and collaboration, ensuring both personal and organisational success. And as such a thriving organisation requires individuals who stand out, embrace their uniqueness, and possess the confidence and vision to make a difference.

When HR professionals within the organisation are engaged, satisfied, and feel valued, they are happier, and as such they foster a positive work environment for employees, which increases overall employee satisfaction.

Employee satisfaction directly impacts how they interact with customers. Happy, engaged employees tend to provide better service, which leads to happier customers. Happier customers are more likely to remain loyal to your brand, increasing repeat business and boosting revenue through customer retention and referrals.

By **positioning** HR effectively, the result is a cumulative effect of happier professionals, employees, and customers, ultimately leading to greater profitability. Engaged and satisfied employees contribute to lower absenteeism and improved operational efficiency. Meanwhile, satisfied customers become more loyal, driving higher revenue and long-term business success.

By **positioning** HR effectively, you not only unlock the potential within the workplace, but you also tap into the deeper insights and wisdom that guide you toward greater success. It's important to listen to that inner voice as it's more than just a fleeting thought; it's your compass, helping you navigate challenges and reach your true purpose. When HR professionals embrace this mindset, they not only align their efforts with the company's goals but also **'Enspire'** That's right **'Enspire'**! You may be wondering what I mean by 'Enspire'? This means that when you are enabled and you are are inspired, you 'Enspire' others, therefore :

Enable + Inspires = 'Enspires' which ='s

Empowerment of self and others better!

This creates a culture of engagement, satisfaction, and loyalty, driving both employee performance and customer success. Ultimately, this leads to a thriving workplace and greater profitability, as both employees and customers become more committed and loyal.

For this to happen, it's essential that each person's purpose and desires are aligned with the company's mission and brought to the forefront. When employees' personal goals resonate with the organisation's vision, it becomes much easier to create meaningful and impactful experiences for everyone. This alignment empowers HR to harness the full potential of each individual, fostering an environment where personal growth and organisational success and growth go hand in hand. When employees feel **connected** to the company's greater purpose, it leads to a culture of empowerment, where everyone is motivated to contribute toward building something extraordinary. In turn, this alignment drives engagement, loyalty, and productivity, enhancing the overall experience for employees, customers, and the company as a whole.

Overcoming fears and transforming negative thoughts is essential to unlocking the fire within you, the passion that drives you forward, **ignites** your creativity, and fuels your determination to excel. In the context of HR, this inner fire propels you to actively align employees' goals with the organisation's mission, creating an environment where everyone feels empowered to contribute their best. By cultivating this passion and hope, you not only elevate yourself but also **'enspire'** those around you, sparking a ripple effect of positivity and motivation within your organisation. So, this means that you are now a **Passionate Advocate**.

When you approach challenges with boldness and confidence, you create an environment where hesitation and procrastination are no longer an option. Being on "death ground" means holding yourself accountable to the consequences of your actions (or inaction) and using that awareness to fuel your drive to succeed. This inner confidence becomes your light, guiding you and others to greatness, as you shine brightly and inspire others to do the same. With passion and hope at the **core** of your being and journey, you foster a belief in what's possible, both for yourself and for your team or others around you. When you bring this mindset to the workplace, it aligns with the company's goals and mission, creating a thriving, empowered team that works together toward extraordinary success.

The mind is your **crown** (head) in action, guiding your thoughts, ideas, and strategies toward a clear purpose. These thoughts manifest through your **core** (heart), where passion, empathy, and purpose reside, fuelling your actions with meaning and intent. Finally, your **contribution** (hands) bring those ideas to life, as you translate vision into tangible results that drive success and innovation within your organisation. By aligning your crown (head), core (heart), and contribution (hands), you create a powerful synergy that propels both personal growth and organisational achievement and growth.

Your **core** (heart) is your magnet as it's the center of your being. It makes you feel whole as you embrace love every day, a love for yourself and others to serve well! This love sets the tone and energy, determining the pulse, mood, and temperature of the people in the company. When your **core** is aligned with your **crown**, it creates a powerful connection that resonates throughout the organisation, **'enspiring'** others to be their best, fostering a culture of engagement, and driving success at all levels. It's about putting people at the heart of the business and giving them a great experience in practice. So that they feel and experience the individual and collective excitement in the growth and achievement of the business.

By harnessing the full potential of your mind, heart, and hands, you transform visions into reality, making a lasting and impactful difference in your workplace. This holistic approach to your work not only elevates your own performance but inspires and empowers others, helping everyone align their goals with the company's mission for collective success. This is what I mean by saying that we profit through championing the implementation of great employee experiences.

> **12**
>
> **Rethink, Reimagine, rebuild and reclaim your values and goals to**

So, transform **crown** by cultivating an attitude that **rethinks, reimagines, rebuilds, and reclaims** your values and goals, so that you are in a better position to **'enspire'** others. This journey is enriched by the growth of your mind, fostering confidence and encouraging you to dive back into the game. As you engage in this process, you'll gain invaluable accomplishments by building remarkable employee experiences. Embrace this evolution with boldness and let your renewed vision and passion guide you to create a workplace where greatness thrives.

Organisationally, it's important to think beyond the moment, not just outside the box! Embrace transcendental moments where you elevate your energy and positivity to new heights, sharing your best self with others. By doing so, you create an inspiring atmosphere that encourages everyone to reach their full potential. These moments of elevated thinking and action become contagious, fostering a culture of innovation, collaboration, and excellence within your organisation.

> ## 13
>
> **Rebuild a stairwell of small wins to create great employee experiences**

It's equally important to **rebuild a stairwell of small wins**, one step at a time, to create great employee experiences through your contribution. Each win builds momentum, strengthening relationships, improving engagement, and setting the stage for meaningful connections. By cultivating these small victories, you prepare yourself and your team for the larger triumphs that come with strong, trusting relationships, especially with your customers. These positive interactions ripple throughout the organisation, reinforcing a culture of excellence and creating an environment where everyone can thrive.

So, great employee experiences are created by the happy HR professional and in turn created by each person in the organisation, especially the leadership in a company. Best companies talk to both the employees and customers as they want to make sure that they know whether their employees and their customers are happy or unhappy. And why is this fundamental?

14

HR Professional first, employee first and customer first!

It is fundamental as all great companies are technically in the customer happiness business so even if they manufacture and sell shoes, they know that they are in the business of making the customer happy and this works 100% of the time. So, **to** run a great people practice within the workplace it needs to be me first, employee first and customer first. If the first two happen well the other will automatically fall into place. Satisfied customers enjoy dealing with business where their team members are happy. Happy team members tend to be more productive and have a long-term commitment to their occupation and the company. So, whether a customer buys from the company or not is often determined by the people in the business. To bring happiness to others, it's essential to treat everyone with kindness. This reflects the timeless principle: "Treat others as you wish to be treated".

Mastering the steps within **The People to Profit Pathway™**, enables you to run a great HR Practice. There are six key steps in this pathway that hold immense significance for human resources and mastering them is essential. Each step is designed to **enable HR** practices, drive organisational success, and create an exceptional employee experience.

By fully understanding and implementing these steps, you can transform your HR approach and make a lasting impact on your organisation's growth and prosperity:

Step 1. Professionalism of HR

By being professional we aim to **enspire** those we lead and provide a service to. Professionalism in HR encompasses a commitment to ethical conduct, competence, effective communication, confidentiality, impartiality, and continuous professional development. Upholding these values and qualities contributes to the credibility, integrity, and effectiveness of HR practices within organisations

By being professional, you use your persona and the power of your profession to **position** HR and Best HR Practice. This clarifies how an HR professional needs to brand themselves and how they need to show up!

For example, HR professionals must handle sensitive information about employees by maintaining confidentiality and exercising proper discretion.

Being professional is not only synonymous with wearing professional attire and using formal language or following strict protocols, as in reality it also encompasses a broader set of qualities and behaviours that go beyond superficial appearances.

True professionalism is about how one conducts themselves, interacts with others, and upholds ethical standards, rather than just adhering to surface-level expectations. Being professional is important as it aims to foster a positive work culture, builds trust, and promotes effective communication and it inspires others who see HR's dedication and excellence.

Step 2. Power of HR

It's about the power of HR Professionals to make strategic decisions and strategic contributions to the people they serve. When it comes to the power of HR you can also think of it as a captain of a ship trying to navigate through a stormy sea.

HR serves as the lookout, scanning the horizon for potential risks and threats and identifying these potential risks and threats to the organisational success and takes proactive measures and looks for opportunities for growth. In times of turbulence and uncertainty, HR demonstrates composure guiding the organisation through rough waters and steering it towards calmer seas and its desired destination of success and growth.

In summary the power of HR is important because it contributes to organisation success, employee satisfaction and engagement, adaptation to change, management and compliance, diversity and inclusion, data -driven decision-making strategic partnering with business leaders and continuous improvement and innovation. By HR **harnessing** **its** **power** **effectively** organisations can create a competitive advantage and achieve sustainable growth.

An example to illustrate the importance of this and the impact of HR's power is in HR conducting employee engagement surveys to gather feedback and to identify areas of improvement in the workplace. As a result, HR introduces comprehensive wellness programs and flexible working arrangements, creating a supportive and adaptable work environment that enhances employee well-being and productivity.

A key misconception about HR's Power is that it is only limited to people related matters and does not extend to other areas of the organisation or that HR's influence is limited to the internal matters of the company and not to the broader stakeholders or community. The truth is that HR has the power to influence strategic decisions, drive change and foster innovation by leveraging its expertise in areas such as business success and competitive advantage.

Step 3. Promotion of HR and Promotion of People

Relates to how human resources presents and **positions** their offering to the people they serve. The promotion of HR involves enhancing the role and influence of Human Resources within an organisation. It includes aligning HR initiatives with business goals, developing HR professionals as strategic leaders, advocating for HR's value through effective communication, fostering collaboration across departments, leveraging data for decision-making, driving change and innovation, prioritising employee engagement and well-being, and championing diversity and inclusion. It aims to position HR as a strategic partner that contributes significantly to organisational success and growth.

The promotion of HR involves those activities and initiatives aimed at elevating the role and influence of the Human

Resources (HR) function within an organisation. This involves highlighting the value that HR brings to the organisation, enhancing its visibility and credibility, and positioning HR as a strategic partner in driving organisational success.

Promotion is essential as it underscores the strategic value HR offers and its vital role in aligning human capital strategies with business objectives. However, HR often faces the challenge of being perceived as merely an administrative function, rather than a revenue generator, with its scope limited to people management. Addressing this misconception is crucial, as the evidence supporting the significance of promoting HR is both clear and compelling. For instance, HR can elevate its profile by implementing initiatives like a comprehensive employee recognition program, demonstrating its impact beyond traditional functions.

In this scenario, HR observes a lack of appreciation and recognition for employees' outstanding contributions, leading to a noticeable decline in engagement and productivity. To address this, HR's promotion initiative involves designing a comprehensive recognition program. This includes communicating and launching the program, providing training and guidelines, clarifying the nominations process, organising the recognition event and awards, and gathering feedback from both management and employees to ensure continuous improvement.

HR professionals must promote HR within the organisation to raise awareness of its strategic value and to drive positive change that contributes to the employee satisfaction levels and overall organisational success.

Step 4. Products of HR

HR products encompass a wide range of services, tools, systems and activities aimed at managing the organisation's workforce effectively, fostering employee engagement and development, and ensuring compliance with legal and regulatory requirements, which are all in the employee lifecycle, ranging from recruitment and selection, to onboarding, performance management, learning and development, talent management and employee engagement initiatives. It's important for these to be aligned to the employee life cycle and touch points.

The products and services of HR are essential for building a high-performing workforce, fostering a positive workplace culture, ensuring legal compliance, and driving organisational success. By investing in HR initiatives and prioritising the needs of employees, organisations can achieve sustainable growth and a competitive advantage in today's dynamic business environment.

HR initiatives such as training and development programs, performance management systems, and employee engagement initiatives contribute to the growth, satisfaction, and motivation of employees. Engaged and skilled employees are more likely to perform well and remain committed to the organisation. By recognising the strategic value of HR products and investing in initiatives that support workforce development and engagement, organisations can unlock the full potential of their employees and gain a competitive advantage in the marketplace.

All the tools that HR makes available to business simplify their practices so that there can be implementation with greater ease. It's important for HR professionals to know which tool to use in relation to which problem and how to tailor this solution back to the specific needs of the business.

Step 5. Packaging of HR and People

The packaging of HR refers to how HR products, services, interventions, initiatives, are presented, communicated, and delivered within the organisation. It involves the design, branding, and presentation of HR offerings to ensure they are aligned to the company branding and are well-received, understood, and effectively utilised by stakeholders, including employees, managers, and senior leadership.

Packaging of HR Products and services is important as it communicates value, increases HR's visibility, enhances relevance, builds credibility, facilitates understanding, drives adoption, supports change management, and enhances overall impact and effectiveness within the organisation.

Effective packaging requires thoughtful consideration and planning throughout the entire lifecycle of HR initiatives, from conception to delivery and beyond. So, creating and defining the HR story within the organisational context and consistently communicating all messages in relation to this story is important. Being able to set great scenes of where the company is right now within the storyline and by providing details that explain the season, the sounds, the visuals and emotions that can be felt, puts the leadership into the scene for them to be keen to know how they can move themselves and their people to acquire greater profit for the company.

HR offerings should be clearly defined, with transparent information provided about their purpose, benefits, and expected outcomes. Clarity helps stakeholders understand the value proposition of HR products and services and encourages buy-in and adoption. HR products and services should be branded and marketed effectively to create a positive perception and generate interest among employees and stakeholders. Consistent messaging and branding helps to establish HR as a trusted partner and resource within the organisation

HR products and services should be easily accessible and user-friendly, with intuitive interfaces and clear instructions provided for stakeholders. Making HR resources readily available and easy to navigate and to promote engagement.

It's important to employ a variety of communication channels to reach different stakeholder groups effectively and to utilise channels such as email, intranet portals, social media, employee newsletters and in person meetings to disseminate HR messages and engage with employees and stakeholders. So, a mix of channels must be used to ensure broad reach and accessibility.

Packaging the HR Story and providing a great employee experience can lead to numerous benefits for employees, the organisation, and its stakeholders. By prioritising the employee experience and effectively communicating the HR story, organisations can create a positive workplace culture, attract top talent, drive performance and achieve long-term success. A positive employee experience with properly packaged HR services, fosters employee satisfaction, engagement, and loyalty thus benefiting the entire organisation.

Step 6· Profit Contribution

Profitability drives business growth, investor confidence, employee satisfaction, community impact, resilience, customer value creation and corporate reputation·

By maximising profitability, business leaders and HR leaders and professionals play a pivotal role in advancing the company's strategic objectives and creating value for all stakeholders and shareholders·

> ### 15
> **Organisations must be equipped with essential principles, innovative strategies, and proven HR best practices**

The contribution of HR professionals to a company's profitability is therefore crucial to its overall success and sustainability·

The use of these foundational elements to guide you to align your HR efforts with business goals to achieve outstanding results includes understanding the link between:

- People and Profit: In other words where organisations need to grasp the direct connection between their workforce (people) and their financial performance (profit)· This involves understanding how employee engagement, productivity, customer satisfaction and other people related factors impact profitability

- *Strategic Human Capital Management: Showing organisations how to strategically manage their human capital is essential.*

- *Measurement and Metrics: Organisations must learn how to identify, measure and track key metrics related to the people-to-profit pathway.*

- *Leadership and culture: Effective leadership and a positive organisational culture are crucial for success along the people-to-profit pathway. Organisations need to teach leaders how to inspire and motivate employees, cultivate a culture of trust and transparency, and lead by example in prioritising people as a strategic asset. Spread some joy by encouraging a culture of celebration! Whether it's small wins or big achievements, a happy workplace is one where victories are cheered on like championship games.*

- *Employee Development and Well-being: Investing in employee development and well-being is essential for maximising the potential of the workforce. Organisations should learn how to provide opportunities for growth and advancement, support employee well-being through wellness programs and work-life balance initiatives and create an inclusive and supportive work environment. Encourage healthy habits as this shows the team that you care about their overall happiness and wellbeing.*

- *Customer Centric approach: Organisations need to adopt a customer-centric mindset and understand the importance of delivering value to customers through their people. This involves teaching employees how their roles contribute to customer satisfaction and how to prioritise customer needs in their daily work.*

- *Continuous improvement and adaptability: The people-to-profit pathway requires organisations to embrace continuous improvement and adaptability. They need to learn how to identify areas for enhancement, experiment with innovative approaches, learn from successes and failures, and adapt to changing market conditions. Allow flexibility in schedules and workflows. A happier workplace understands that life happens, and sometimes, a little flexibility can make all the difference.*

- *Communication and collaboration: Effective communication and collaboration are essential for success along the people-to-profit pathway. Organisations need to teach employees how to communicate openly and transparently, collaborate across teams and departments, and share knowledge and best practices to drive innovation. Teamwork makes the dream work so it is important to encourage collaboration and camaraderie among team members when everyone feels like they are part of a supportive community they flourish.*

- *Ethical and responsible practices: Organisations must adhere to ethical and responsible practices in all aspects of their operations, including how they manage their people. This involves treating employees fairly and with respect, promoting diversity and inclusion, and upholding principles of social responsibility and sustainability*

- *Alignment with business goals: Organisations need to ensure that their efforts along the people-to-profit pathway are aligned with overarching business goals and objectives. This involves setting clear targets, measuring progress towards those targets, and adjusting as needed to stay on course*

- *Practicing Gratitude: Take a moment to appreciate the trivial things as gratitude goes a long way in fostering a positive atmosphere. Plus, who does not love a heartfelt thank you now and then.*

The challenge I often notice is that HR professionals sometimes struggle to effectively brand and position themselves, as well as the HR profession, due to a few key elements that might be missing.

Another challenge I see is that HR Professionals often do not create a consistent image of growth and are as such not always able to remain ahead of the curve. By this I mean that they don't always build a compelling case about their contribution and the approach they apply in preparing the organisation for the future workforce and world of work. This can have an impact on their credibility and capability. It is therefore critical for HR to build and communicate a compelling HR strategic approach based on best practice and not simply on procedures.

Another challenge I often observe is that HR divisions may not always include the most impactful metrics on their dashboards, making it harder to showcase their true value and contribution to the company's bottom line. So, you may find value in using the people to profit pathway as an approach in that enables :

- HR professionals to partner with the Internal communication through a dedicated resource to develop and implement their personal branding and positioning. Employees are then constantly and consistently aware of the HR Professional interventions and the role they would need to play to participate.

- HR Professionals to align the company customer value proposition with the employee value proposition.

- HR professionals to showcase their impact on the bottom line through a return-on-investment approach. This not only strengthens the company's market positioning against competitors but also enables and empowers HR to drive skill development, align the company's life cycle with its culture, and craft a compelling narrative of organisational success.

- HR professionals to reference and use some of the correct metrics.

As such HR professionals are shown how to:

- Better **position** HR through a better understanding of the company they serve.
- How to **develop** their skills to align with the company life cycle to the company culture and to tell a compelling story
- To include HR reports that always reference **people as assets** and the impact they have on the profits of the company or to the service of the institution whether it is a corporate, non-profit or government institution.
- **Position** themselves better based on an assessment of their own capability and understanding of the company culture

Remember the picture I mentioned you should always have in mind and keep in your back pocket? Now, let's dive deeper into the financial benefits of this straightforward code, as it links the satisfaction and enablement of HR professionals and employees to overall company success, including profitability:

The code is:

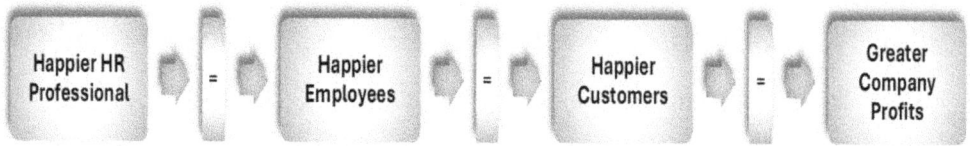

So, linking key financial indicators to key HR metrics especially, related to employee experience can showcase HR's strategic role in driving financial outcomes, and as such reinforcing its value beyond the traditional administrative functions. These metrics include:

o Sales per employee

o Revenue growth, profit margins,

o Customer and Employee Satisfaction ratio'

o Return on investment (ROI), and shareholder value provide direct evidence of the impact of employee experience on business profitability.

o Compensation of employment metrics, which include measures related to employee compensation and benefits, play a crucial role in the relationship between employee experience and company profitability.

This relates to the Cost of employment ratio to company budget as per the **Employment to Budget Ratio** ratio formula below:

Formula for Employment to Budget Ratio:
Total Employment Costs /Total Budget×100 e.g.

Budget: 1000 000

Employment costs: 630 000.

Percentage Cost: 63%. The lower this percentage, the greater the cost savings and as a result an improvement in the profit levels.

Key Components:

- Total Employment Costs: Includes salaries, wages, bonuses, benefits, payroll taxes, and training expenses.
- Total Budget: The overall financial plan covering all expenses, including operational, capital, and administrative costs.

Why It Matters ?

- It helps organisations evaluate workforce cost efficiency.
- Assists in budgeting and workforce planning.
- Provides insight into labor-intensive vs. capital-intensive business models.

A **high ratio** suggests a labor-intensive structure, while a **low ratio** may indicate automation, outsourcing, or lower labor costs relative to overall spending.

Like the net contribution margin figure this is the number one figure that needs to be looked at for the success of any business from an HR perspective.

The **Net Contribution Margin** is a measure of how much revenue remains after covering variable costs, which can then contribute to covering fixed costs and generating profit. It is calculated as:

Net Contribution Margin:

Total Revenue—Total Variable Costs

or expressed as a percentage:

Net Contribution Margin %:

Total Revenue—Total Variable Costs/Total Revenue) x100

Key Components:

- **Revenue:** Total income from sales.

- **Variable Costs:** Costs that change with production levels (e.g., raw materials, direct labor, sales commissions).

- **Fixed Costs** (not included in contribution margin): Costs that remain constant regardless of production levels (e.g., rent, salaries, insurance).

Why It Matters ?

- It helps businesses determine pricing strategies.

- Assists in break-even analysis.

- Shows how much each sale contributes to covering fixed costs and generating profit.

o Increased Productivity = Cost Savings and Higher Revenue When HR professionals feel engaged and valued, they are more productive and motivated to deliver their best work. Productivity improvements across an organisation mean tasks are completed faster and more efficiently, reducing operational costs. For example, projects may be completed ahead of schedule, which not only saves on labour costs but also allows companies to allocate resources to other value-adding activities, driving potential revenue growth. Additionally, happier professionals often inspire innovation. When employees are motivated, they tend to think more creatively, leading to new products, services, or processes that can boost revenue.

o Turnover rates: reduced Turnover = Lower Recruitment and Training Costs High employee retention is one of the biggest cost-saving advantages of having happy, engaged professionals. When your HR professionals help foster a positive work environment, employees are more likely to stay with the company long-term. This saves the business money on recruitment and training, which can be expensive. The cost to replace an employee can range from 50% to 200% of their annual salary due to recruitment fees, training costs, and lost productivity during the transition period.

- *Improved Employee Satisfaction = Enhanced Customer Service* Employee satisfaction has a direct impact on customer satisfaction. Happy employees who feel valued are more likely to go the extra mile for customers, resulting in better customer service. When customers receive excellent service, they are more likely to become repeat buyers, leave positive reviews, and refer others to your company, all of which increases revenue.

- *Employee engagement scores, Engagement = Reduced Absenteeism and Operational Efficiency.* A satisfied and engaged workforce also leads to reduced absenteeism. When employees are happier, they are less likely to take unnecessary sick days, which means less disruption to business operations. Reduced absenteeism leads to more consistent output and less need for temporary staff or costly overtime.

- *Customer satisfaction ratings: Customer loyalty = Higher Long-Term Revenue* Satisfied employees foster better customer relationships, which in turn builds brand loyalty.

Loyal customers are more likely to make repeat purchases, refer new clients, and provide positive word-of-mouth marketing, which is invaluable and comes at no extra cost to the company. According to research, it costs five times more to acquire a new customer than to retain an existing one, so focusing on employee satisfaction is an investment that pays off in the form of loyal, long-term customers.

Let's explore specific calculations that illustrate the impact of improving employee satisfaction. How this can directly impact on a company's bottom line. These examples will quantify the financial benefits of specific initiatives.

1. Reducing Turnover Costs

Scenario:

- Company size: 500 employees

- Average salary: $60,000

- Annual turnover rate: 15% (75 employees leave per year)

- Cost to replace one employee: 100% of annual salary ($60,000)

Calculation:

- Total turnover cost = 75 employees × 60,000=4.5 million annually.

Initiative: Implement recognition programs and stay interviews to reduce turnover by 5%.

- New turnover rate: 10% (50 employees leave per year).

- New turnover cost = 50 employees × 60,000= 3 million annually.

Savings:

- 4.5million−3 million = **$1.5 million saved annually.**

2. Increasing Productivity

Scenario:

- Engaged employees are **17% more productive** (Gallup).

- Average revenue per employee: $200,000.

Calculation:

- Current productivity = 500 employees × $200,000 = $100 million annually

- Increased productivity = $100 million × 1.17 = $117 million annually

- Additional revenue = $117 million - $100 million = $17 million annually

3. Lowering Absenteeism Costs

Scenario:

- Average absenteeism rate: 4% (20 days per employee per year).

- Average daily wage: 240(240(60,000 ÷ 250 working days).

- Cost of absenteeism per employee = 20 days x 240=4,800 annually.

Initiative: Introduce wellness programs and flexible work arrangements to reduce absenteeism by 1%.

- New absenteeism rate: 3% (15 days per employee per year).

- New cost of absenteeism per employee = 15 days x 240=3,600 annually.

Savings:

- 4,800—3,600 = **$1,200 saved per employee annually.**

- Total savings = 500 employees x 1,200=600,000 annually.

4. Improving Customer Retention

Scenario:

- Current customer retention rate: 80%.

- Average customer lifetime value (CLV): $10,000.

- Number of customers: 1,000.

Initiative: Improve employee satisfaction to boost customer service, increasing retention by 5%.

- New retention rate: 85%.

- Additional customers retained = 1,000 × 5% = 50 customers.

- Additional revenue = 50 customers × 10,000=500,000 annually.

5. Attracting Top Talent

Scenario:

- Cost to recruit and train a new employee: $10,000.

- Number of new hires per year: 50.

- Total recruitment cost = 50 × 10,000=500,000 annually.

Initiative: Build a strong employer brand to reduce recruitment costs by 20%.

- Current recruitment cost per employee: $10,000
- Reduction in recruitment cost: 20% of $10,000 = $2,000
- New recruitment cost per employee: $10,000 - $2,000 = $8,000
- Total number of hires annually: 50
- Total recruitment cost after reduction: 50 × $8,000 = $400,000 annually

Savings:

- 500,000–400,000 = **$100,000** saved annually

6. Reducing Healthcare Costs

Scenario:

- Average annual healthcare cost per employee: $10,000.

- Total healthcare cost = 500 employees × 10,000=5 million annually.

- Current healthcare cost per employee: $10,000
- Reduction in healthcare cost: 5% of $10,000 = $500
- New healthcare cost per employee: $10,000 - $500 = $9,500
- Total number of employees: 500
- Total healthcare cost after reduction: 500 × $9,500 = $4.75 million annually

Savings:

- *5million—4·75 million = **$250,000** saved annually·*

7· Boosting Revenue Through Innovation

Scenario:

- *Engaged employees are more likely to contribute innovative ideas·*

- *Assume 1% of employees generate ideas that lead to new revenue streams·*

- *Average revenue from one innovation: $500,000·*

Calculation:

- *Number of innovators = 500 × 1% = 5 employees·*

- *Total additional revenue = 5 × 500,000=2·5 million annually*

8· Improving Employee Engagement: Scenario:

- *Current engagement rate: 60% (300 engaged employees)·*

- *Engaged employees generate 21% higher profitability (Gallup)·*

- *Average profit per employee: $50,000·*

Initiative: *Increase engagement rate to 70% (350 engaged employees).*

- *Additional engaged employees = 50.*

- *Additional profit per engaged employee = 50,000 x 21% = 10,500*

- *Total additional profit = 50 employees x $10,500 = $525,000 annually.*

Summary of Financial Impact

Initiative	Annual Savings/Revenue
Reducing turnover by 5%	$1.5 million
Increasing productivity by 17%	$17 million
Lowering absenteeism by 1%	$600,000
Improving customer retention by 5%	$500,000
Reducing recruitment costs by 20%	$100,000
Lowering healthcare costs by 5%	$250,000
Boosting revenue through innovation	$2.5 million
Increasing engagement by 10%	$525,000
Total	**$23.075 million**

By implementing employee satisfaction initiatives, the company in this example could potentially save or generate **over $23 million annually**. These calculations demonstrate how investing in employees directly translates to **improved profitability** and a stronger bottom line.

Highly engaged employees contribute directly to a company's financial success. Organisations with strong employee engagement see 21% higher profitability and outperform competitors by up to 147% in earnings per share (Gallup). Employee satisfaction boosts productivity, enhances customer loyalty, and reduces costly turnover. High retention rates preserve institutional knowledge, ensuring smoother workflows and minimizing recruitment and training expenses. Engaged employees also drive operational efficiency by taking initiative, improving processes, and fostering collaboration. HR plays a crucial role in measuring and leveraging these engagement metrics to demonstrate its value, guiding decision-making that strengthens both workforce morale and the company's bottom line.

Investing in employee engagement goes beyond creating a positive work environment as it drives long-term success by boosting productivity, reducing costs, enhancing customer satisfaction, and increasing profitability. A happy workforce leads to tangible financial gains, strengthening the company's bottom line. Additionally, embracing workplace culture and its unique quirks fosters a sense of belonging, making work feel like a second home. Here are some suggested Key Performance Indicators (KPIs) that can help measure the success and impact of HR professionals, employee satisfaction, and customer experience, ultimately leading to increased profitability:

1. Employee Engagement & Satisfaction KPIs

- *Employee Engagement Score:* Measured through regular surveys to assess how engaged employees feel in their roles.

- *Job Satisfaction Rate:* Collected through pulse surveys or annual satisfaction surveys to determine overall employee morale.

- *Employee Retention Rate:* The percentage of employees who stay with the company over a specific period. A high retention rate indicates satisfaction.

- *Turnover Rate:* The percentage of employees who leave the organization, especially in key positions. Lower turnover signifies higher employee satisfaction.

- *Employee Net Promoter Score (eNPS):* Measures how likely employees are to recommend your company as a place to work. A positive eNPS shows that employees are satisfied and engaged.

2. Productivity & Efficiency KPIs

- Absenteeism Rate: Track how often employees are absent. Lower absenteeism rates indicate higher engagement and well-being.
- Training Completion Rate: The percentage of employees who complete their required training on time, which can affect skill development and productivity.
- Time to Fill Open Roles: A measure of how quickly open positions are filled. Faster hiring reflects efficient processes and a positive workplace reputation.

3. Customer Experience KPIs

- Customer Satisfaction Score (CSAT): A measure of how satisfied customers are with the service they receive, often linked to employee satisfaction.
- Net Promoter Score (NPS): Indicates how likely customers are to recommend your company, reflecting the quality of customer service.
- Customer Retention Rate: The percentage of customers who return to do business with you over a specified period. High retention is often linked to better customer service.

- *Customer Complaints Resolution Time: The average time it takes to resolve a customer complaint. A faster resolution time indicates a well-engaged and responsive team. Sales per Customer: The revenue generated per customer. Happier customers often make more purchases, increasing this KPI.*

Points to Ponder:

What strategies have you used to showcase the direct impact of successful HR interventions on the company's bottom line? For e.g. a correlation between the customer satisfaction index outcomes to the Employee satisfaction Index outcomes. While not every company explicitly breaks down HR-related metrics in their financial statements, many include narrative descriptions or management discussions in their annual reports that highlight strategic HR initiatives and their expected or realised impact on financial performance. These disclosures help investors, stakeholders, and analysts understand how human capital management practices contribute to the company's overall value creation and sustainability.

*Focusing on Return on Investment (ROI) calculations for HR interventions and programs is essential for **Positioning** HR and demonstrating its value add.*

Here's an example of some of the common questions and responses related to ROI:

- **Q: What is ROI in the context of HR interventions? A:** ROI (Return on Investment) in HR interventions measures the financial return gained from HR programs relative to their cost. It helps determine the effectiveness and value of HR activities, such as training, recruitment, or employee wellness programs.

- **Q: What factors should be considered when calculating ROI for HR programs? A:** Factors include the direct costs of the program, indirect costs, measurable benefits (like increased productivity or reduced turnover), and intangible benefits (like improved employee morale).

- **Q: How do you calculate ROI for an HR intervention? A:** The basic ROI formula is:

  ROI % = Net Benefit Cost of Intervention / Cost of HR Intervention × 100

Where the Net Benefit is the difference between the financial gains from the intervention and the cost of the intervention.

- **Q: Can you provide an example of ROI calculation for a training program?** A company invests **$50,000** in a leadership development training program for its managers.

After six months, the company observes the following benefits:

- o Increased productivity leads to an additional **$120,000 in revenue**

- o Reduced employee turnover saves **$30,000 hiring onboarding costs**

Step 1: Calculate the Net Benefit

Net Benefit= (Financial Gains+Cost Savings) −Cost of Training

= (120,000+30,000) −50,000

= (120,000 + 30,000) - 50,000= (120,000+30,000) 50,000

=150,000−50,000=100,000

Step 2: Apply the ROI Formula

ROI (%) = (Net Benefit / Cost of Training) ×100

ROI (%) = (100,000/50,000) ×100

ROI (%) = 200%

So, the overall **positioning** of Human Resources is all about creating and promoting a consistent image of growth considering the **6 elements of professionalism, power, product packaging and profit·** It's also about establishing a specific place or niche in the minds of both the employer and the employee, on the growth path of both the company and the individual·

It's also about effectively communicating the benefits and value that HR provides. Establishing a consistent image of growth is essential in positioning HR offerings or services, ensuring that both the company's and the employee's growth are clearly highlighted through positive employee experiences.

Business growth is directly tied to people growth. HR professionals must effectively position their value through clear messaging, visual elements, and impactful reporting to engage leadership and employees in HR initiatives.

The **People to Profit Pathway™©** provides a structured approach to packaging the HR story, aligning it with company culture and lifecycle. It helps HR professionals craft compelling reports and dashboards that highlight HR's strategic contribution to business success.

By mastering expert positioning and clear communication, HR can ensure leadership understands its role in fostering a positive employee experience. Employees, in turn, become active participants in HR-driven solutions, reinforcing HR's influence beyond traditional administrative functions. So, to successfully navigate the people-to-profit pathway, organisations must be equipped with essential principles, innovative strategies, and proven best practices.

When HR professionals feel engaged, valued, and fulfilled in their roles, their enthusiasm drives higher productivity and innovation. A motivated HR team not only works more efficiently but also introduces creative solutions that enhance business operations. This can lead to faster project completion, cost savings, and increased revenue. For example, an engaged HR team might implement a digital recruitment tool that reduces hiring time by half, optimizing resources and accelerating business growth. Similarly, in a retail setting, engaged employees go above and beyond for customers, creating positive experiences that strengthen brand loyalty.

When HR professionals feel engaged, valued, and fulfilled in their roles, their enthusiasm drives higher productivity and innovation. A motivated HR team not only works more efficiently but also introduces creative solutions that enhance business operations. This can lead to faster project completion, cost savings, and increased revenue. For example, an engaged HR team might implement a digital recruitment tool that reduces hiring time by half, optimizing resources and accelerating business growth. Similarly, in a retail setting, engaged employees go above and beyond for customers, creating positive experiences that strengthen brand loyalty. Creating a happier workplace is an ongoing journey and is therefore not a one-time event. The journey from people to profitability is like a symphony orchestra, where leadership acts as the conductor, guiding employees, each with their unique skills, toward a shared goal. Just as a well-coordinated orchestra creates a masterpiece, a well-managed organisation thrives through teamwork, leadership, and collaboration. The People to Profit Pathway helps HR professionals move from uncertainty to confidently positioning HR as a key business driver, demonstrating its commercial value and enhancing both employee and client satisfaction. As HR Leaders and HR professionals, our role is akin to that of a workplace champion, where we empower colleagues and guide the organisation towards growth and innovation with empathy, responsibility, and humility. Understanding the evolution of HR from traditional personnel management to becoming a critical strategic partner underscores the dynamic role HR professionals now play. By developing a Strategic Roadmap that focuses on clear goals, gain, guidance, and growth, HR professionals can elevate their practice to create long-lasting organisational impact.

Financially, the benefits are significant. Engaged employees are more productive, which reduces costs and increases revenue. Higher employee satisfaction reduces turnover, saving on recruitment and training costs, while happier employees lead to happier customers, increasing brand loyalty and driving repeat business. By mastering this journey where you combining professionalism, strategic alignment, and continuous improvement, HR professionals will not only enhance the workplace experience but also ensure sustained growth and profitability for the organisation. It's a transformational path that empowers HR to become a pivotal driver of business success.

So, take this opportunity to lead with purpose, foster positive change, and create a thriving workplace where both people and the company flourish together.

By continuously nurturing HR team members and embracing a culture of growth and positivity, you set the stage for a thriving workplace where everyone feels valued and empowered.

16

Keep Striving, keep growing and watch your workplace flourish

---

Keep striving, keep growing, and watch your workplace flourish like never before. Let this chapter be a testament to the transformative power of great HR practices and the endless possibilities they unlock for your organisation.

Ultimately, HR needs to **enable** its own growth and impact, ensuring that both employees and the organisation thrive together.

A Point to Ponder:

A great employee experience helps you to move the needle on HR's overall business impact! And interestingly enough: A great employee experience can be accessible to all people through your contribution as happy HR Leaders and Professionals and business leaders. Isn't that just fantastic!

"I've learned that people will forget what you said, people will forget what you did, but people will never forget how you made them feel" Maya Angelo

Chapter Four

Leveraging Your Voice for Greater Engagement

HR professionals need to leverage the use of their voice for greater transformation as presentations are powerful engagement tools. HR professionals need to therefore seize every presentation opportunity, not only to deliver a compelling message but also to create powerful engagement. Presenting for powerful engagement means using your V·O·I·C·E to craft presentations that captivate and inspire, drawing everyone in to recognise the importance of a better employee experience. By leveraging your V·O·I·C·E, you can deliver presentations that are not only engaging but also uplifting, ensuring that the message resonates deeply and encourages meaningful understanding. So, what I mean by V·O·I·C·E is :

- the **Variety** you bring in your voice,
- how you **optimise** your voice during delivery of a presentation and engagement,

- how you vary your pitch patterns for better **Intonation**, and how you
- bring **clarity** where your voice is crisp and easily understood and through
- **engagement** you have great expression as you use the platform and movements that express confidence.

These five elements are important especially when you need to shift the beliefs and mindset of your audience whilst presenting for buy in or to win them over. This we know is crucial, as their beliefs directly influence their feelings. So, to minimise resistance when trying to change a belief, these shifts need to happen subtly, without the audience being consciously aware. So, leveraging your V.O.I.C.E for engagement are important steps for HR Professionals who are looking to elevate their presentations and engage their audience or client in a way that makes a lasting impact.

In essence, the goal is to change their mindset in a way that feels like a natural part of their routine, whilst making them shift to new behaviours. This can be achieved by crafting your message in a way that deeply resonates with them, using stories, analogies, and visual aids to gently guide their thinking. By aligning your narrative with their values and experiences, you can nudge your audience towards new perspectives and actions without triggering defensiveness. Remember, as you present to your audience, their minds are creating internal images and dialogues as they process your message.

So, to paint a clear picture in their minds, leverage vivid imagery and descriptive language. Engage their senses and emotions by incorporating relatable scenarios and examples, making your message not just heard, but felt. This approach helps your audience internalise your points more effectively, as they connect your ideas with their own thoughts and experiences, enhancing their ability to shift their perspectives. In so doing your client listens and responds positively to your suggested HR Interventions.

When presenting, it's essential to recognise that some individuals may be at a crossroads or in need of guidance. So, the way you communicate with them can have a profound impact on their emotional state. Whether they're experiencing uncertainty or hesitation, how you present information can influence their perception of their ability to take action. So, to help them make the right decision or take the necessary steps, you may need to guide them in shifting how they view themselves, specifically their capabilities, strengths, and potential for growth.

For them to take the right actions, especially when this involves stepping outside of one's comfort zone, can often be a daunting and a fear-inducing experience. The internal process of visualising this change, what it looks like, what it entails, and how it affects them can create anxiety. This is because they may not yet see themselves as someone capable of making that change or taking those next steps. However, the key to easing this fear is in providing clarity. When people can clearly see the path ahead and understand what's required of them, it helps them feel more confident and in control.

So, to facilitate this, always provide a clear, step-by-step visual roadmap that outlines exactly what actions need to be taken as you present. This roadmap should not only break down the process into manageable chunks but also emphasize the importance of each step. When individuals can clearly see the steps ahead, they're more likely to feel empowered and motivated to take the next action. This clarity removes uncertainty and offers a sense of direction. Additionally, visualising the desired outcome, how their efforts will lead to success or growth then reinforces the importance of their actions and fuels their drive to move forward. This approach helps shift your audience from fear and hesitation to a state of empowered readiness, enabling them to make confident decisions and take the right actions. By breaking down the process into manageable steps and illustrating the positive outcomes of each action, you can make the path forward less daunting and more achievable. This approach helps your audience see the value and feasibility of the changes, fostering confidence and their commitment to how they receive the message from your presentation. Therefore, to develop a pattern of gain where your client buys into your services or the intervention that you need to recommend and implement, you must propose the right actions to be taken and implemented, for them to get the results they want. The way you present, and influence business leaders will determine whether they remain with the status quo or choose to elevate their approach and operate at a higher level. This, in turn, will influence whether they take the necessary steps to support the proposed intervention. Gaining their buy-in for your services or initiatives is crucial, as it encourages them to recognise the need for change and commit to achieving greater success. When a client rejects your proposed intervention or service, it creates a cycle of discomfort. This discomfort can manifest in several ways:

o **Indecision,** where the audience hesitates to evolve their beliefs.
o **Opposition,** where they resist change to retain control.
o **Postponement,** where they put off decisions indefinitely.
o **Avoidance,** where they stay preoccupied to sidestep the issue.

All the above patterns will continue to give the results that the business does not necessarily want, meaning that you are remaining in a pattern of pain. Whenever you present, do so in such a way that you see the incremental changes. It's important for you to therefore trust your process and invest your time in it.

The challenge I see in HR Professionals presenting is that we have not received adequate presentation skills training to be a presence on the platform from the onset, as we need to promote and pitch HR from the outset. We also don't know how to use our V·O·I·C·E as a launchpad that would help to change our clients' patterns of belief in a way that would enhance HR services to them. This gap in training leaves HR Professionals at a disadvantage, as they struggle to effectively communicate their value and how to better influence key stakeholders. To bridge this gap, it's crucial to invest in comprehensive presentation skills development, empowering HR professionals to confidently convey their messages, inspire change, and drive impactful outcomes within their organisations. By mastering these skills, they can transform their interactions, build stronger relationships, and significantly enhance their overall service delivery.

HR Professionals can, therefore, be provided with the opportunity to craft a compelling presentation using a framework that will assist them in garnering buy-in of all relevant leadership and stakeholders where the HR offering is adequately promoted.

So, activating the 5 elements in V·O·I·C·E , is in essence, a framework that can be used to take your presenting outcomes to the next level as you capture the attention of the audience and you are able to get better engagement and their buy in support of your proposed intervention., in a way that is captivating and based on real-life stories of the people in the company.

17
Capture the attention of the audience for engagement and buy in

V·O·I·C·E within the Launchpad is all about the deliberate use of vocal techniques, coupled with enthusiasm and eye contact to captivate your audience and leave a lasting impression.

Variety
Voice variety refers to the range and diversity with which you speak. It includes elements like tone, pitch, volume, speed, and emphasis, and it's essential for effective communication. Mastering voice variety means being able to adjust these elements thoughtfully, depending on the emotion, intention, or message you want to convey.

Having a varied voice keeps your audience engaged by breaking the monotony, ensuring that they remain attentive and connected to your message. It adds richness to your delivery, helping to highlight key points, convey different emotions, and maintain interest throughout your presentation. Whether in public speaking, acting, or any scenario where communication is key, voice variety is crucial. It prevents your speech from sounding flat or robotic, making your message more compelling.

In the context of presenting, voice variety is about modulation, adjusting your tone, pitch, and volume in response to the needs of the moment and your audience. It's a powerful tool that not only enhances clarity but also increases the emotional impact of what you're saying, ensuring that your delivery aligns with the energy of your message. By engaging in voice modulation, you prevent your presentation from feeling predictable, creating a dynamic experience that resonates with your listeners.

Variety in your voice enhances your ability to connect with your audience, adding depth and expression to your communication. Mastering this skill keeps engagement high and leaves a lasting impact. So, make use of a variety of voices in a way that makes it beneficial to promote a flexible, adaptable, and individualised approach to understanding and pursuing purpose.

As much as you need variety in your voice, it would help if you also had variety in your stance, as it gives or sends off signals about your confidence. So, to master a proper stance, always stand in front of the stage or in front of your audience with your legs hip-width apart.

A misconception about voice variety is that it only involves changing the pitch or volume of ' 'one's voice. And it's all about being loud and dramatic. Voice variety however, encompasses and is about using vocal modulation skilfully to enhance communication and connecting with the audience.

Optimise

Optimising your voice for clarity means taking steps to ensure that your speech is easily understood and understandable to others. Here are some ways you can achieve clarity in your vocal communication. Use your tone of voice for clarity and variety. Talk to your speaking voice and adjust the volume of your voice depending on the room acoustics and the audience size. Optimising your voice for clarity is essential because it ensures that your message is easily understood by others, keeping them engaged and building trust and rapport.

When it comes to optimising your voice, think of it as tuning an instrument. Just like a musician adjusts strings, keys, and airflow to produce the desired sound, you can adapt your pitch, tone, pace, and articulation to create clear, engaging, and expressive communication.

By mastering these elements, you can effectively convey your message, captivate your audience, and achieve your communication goals.

Intonation

It involves the rise and fall of pitch patterns across phrases, sentences, or paragraphs. Intonation plays a crucial role in conveying meaning, emotion, and emphasis in your presentation.

In conveying meaning, you are in a state of flow, especially where you are making important points and where your peripheral vision and your parasympathetic cells are renewing your harmonious state. You engage your unconscious mind where the message is delivered through you and not from you and your primary focus is through your eyes and your state relates to your heart.

Your lungs help you to remain calm and relaxed because of your breathing. Your peripheral vision also allows you to multi-focus. When you go into peripheral vision, everything is less intense as you have a greater or bigger perspective, and you move into a pure creative thinking state when you trust the moment and the message.

Peripheral vision needs practice if you want to remain within the state of flow, so it's important to be in a state of calm and relaxation through breathing in a standard, regular pattern. Moving into foveal vision immediately would narrow your vision, so it is better to remain in peripheral vision so that you do not go into stress.

Mastering intonation can significantly enhance one's ability to communicate clearly and persuasively. A common misconception about intonation is that it solely depends on the rise and fall of pitch at the end of a sentence, particularly in the context of asking questions.

Clarity

Clarity of voice refers to the degree to which speech is easily understood and intelligible to listeners. A clear voice is crisp, articulate, and free from distortion or ambiguity. Here are some critical aspects of clarity of voice: annunciation, articulation, volume, and rate of speech. Clarity of Voice in articulation so that the audience can follow your message without confusion. This clarity also includes your storyline and responses to questions that you are asked.

Engagement, expression, and eye contact means that the presenter needs to be engaged by standing in front of the platform of engagement, and all movements must be expressed in a way that shows confidence. There are several types of movement of confidence: neutral, sovereign, sage, lover, and warrior.

The movements can be neutral, where your hands are clasped together in front of you, or sovereign, where your hand moves down from your belt line, indicating that you mean what you are saying, Sage, where your hand is on your chin and arm, crossed, especially when being asked a question and where you want to be considered as ethical.

It's important to smile while talking and to make eye contact by randomly selecting people in the audience, look directly in their eyes, hold eye contact until you reach a natural pause. Create memorable and meaningful experiences that leave a lasting impression on the audience and drive them to act or change their perspective in some way. It requires a combination of practical communication skills, audience awareness, and strategic planning to achieve desired outcomes and make a meaningful impact by keeping them actively involved and invested in the content being presented and influencing their thoughts, emotions, and behaviours. While giving a presentation, always build up to the point before you share it!

> **18**
>
> **Always build up to the point before you share it!**

Your presentation slides are best depicted in pictures and less in words and as such, it is best to avoid bullet points. Use pictures as they describe a thousand words. Handling of questions: Acknowledge them nonverbally, continue speaking without changing content flow, take a question only when you are ready, not when they ask it, and give your answer to the whole audience.

Remember, questions lead to more questions, so questions are best left to the end so ask your audience to raise your hand if they need any points of clarity at the end.

I cannot emphasise the importance of practising and using other colleagues to master the delivery of presentations enough as Human Resources professionals need to be confident whilst they present and to be able to influence their audience to the point of buy-in and for the necessary changes to beliefs, actions or decisions that need to take place.

Another problem I see is that HR Professionals are not able to communicate ' 'HR's value proposition effectively and in a way that captivates and provides for a remarkable story. HR Professionals also need to often use presentations opportunities to leverage engagement and tell a story to win their customers over. The consequence of that is lost opportunities for HR to facilitate engagement for, more significant, more incredible company results and profit when engaging leadership and executives in the business.

Learning how to harness the power of engagement through mastering the five key steps of this system is essential for any HR professional who aims to excel in running their HR practice. By fully understanding and implementing these steps, they can elevate their communication, drive greater impact, and lead their teams and organisations with confidence and clarity.

By following through on the 5-step process, HR professionals will not only delight and inspire the customer but also engage them for the correct result. This approach also provides you with the opportunity to practice until you have mastered this art of presenting.

So, the approach shows you how to focus while you are presenting and to be yourself. It also shows you how to stand in front of your audience, what is vital about body language and how to use your voice. It also shows you the approach you need to take to deliver your message. Adapting your speaking style during a presentation needs your voice for projection, expression, and authenticity. So, it's crucial that you pay attention to your posture and your body alignment.

The Benefit of using this approach is that you are shown how to present in practice as you are given the opportunity to apply the skills that you are taught.

So, thinking about your voice as a multifaceted instrument for communication, expression, influence, self-reflection, and connection can help you develop a more nuanced and practical approach to vocal expression in your personal and professional life.

Effective presentations require a dynamic approach to voice, body language, and engagement. Voice modulation is about adjusting your tone, pitch, and volume which enhances clarity and emotional impact, keeping the audience engaged. Just like tuning an instrument, optimising your voice clarity involves articulation, pacing, and breathing control.

Intonation, the rise and fall of pitch, conveys meaning and emotion, while peripheral vision helps maintain a calm, creative state during delivery. Clear articulation and confident body language, such as stance and movement, reinforce credibility. Presenters should use visuals over text-heavy slides, maintain eye contact, and handle questions strategically.

HR professionals must master storytelling to communicate HR's value effectively, driving engagement and business impact. A structured, five-step approach to presenting can enhance their influence, helping them deliver compelling messages that inspire action. By refining these skills through practice, HR professionals can confidently showcase their expertise and drive meaningful change.

When it comes to delivering powerful presentations as an HR professional, connecting with your audience and engaging them in a meaningful way is crucial· Here are some best practices that can help you elevate your presentation skills using the V·O·I·C·E framework for engagement·

- **Define Your Audience**

The foundation of any successful presentation lies in understanding who you are speaking to· Whether you're addressing senior leadership, employees, or external clients, it's important to tailor your message to their needs, expectations, and level of understanding· For example, executives might be more interested in how HR strategies directly impact business growth and profitability, whereas employees might be more engaged by hearing how these strategies will improve their day-to-day experience·

By defining your audience, you can craft a message that resonates with their interests and concerns· This approach not only helps maintain their attention but also ensures that your message feels relevant and actionable· It's all about connecting on their level and addressing what matters most to them·

- **Use Storytelling: A Powerful Tool**

One of the most engaging ways to present is through storytelling· People are wired to respond to stories that are relatable, memorable, and can evoke emotion, making your message stick· Instead of presenting dry facts or data, weave these elements into a narrative that brings your points to life. For instance, if you're discussing an HR initiative, share a success story of how it impacted employee engagement or retention. Talk about the challenges, the strategies implemented, and the positive outcomes.

Storytelling transforms complex or abstract ideas into something tangible and relatable. By humanizing the data, you'll not only keep your audience engaged but also make your message much more impactful.

- **Foster Interaction and Engagement**

A key aspect of any effective presentation is interaction. Encourage your audience to participate by asking questions, invite feedback, or present scenarios for them to consider. This creates a two-way conversation rather than a one-sided lecture. By involving your audience, you ensure they remain engaged and actively think about the content you're presenting.

Interaction also provides real-time insights into how well your message is resonating. If your audience asks follow-up questions or provides feedback, you can adjust your presentation on the spot to clarify points or dive deeper into areas of interest. This adaptability demonstrates confidence and responsiveness, both of which strengthen your credibility as a speaker.

- **Provide Clear Takeaways and Action Steps**

Every effective presentation should conclude with clear, actionable takeaways. After sharing your key points, make sure to summarize them and provide specific next steps your audience can take. This could involve implementing a new HR strategy, adopting a particular mindset, or simply reflecting on a change they need to make in their approach. The goal is to ensure that your presentation doesn't just end when you stop speaking. A strong call to action encourages your audience to continue engaging with the ideas you've presented and to take tangible steps to apply them. This is where your message can have a lasting impact, beyond the moment of the presentation itself.

- **Optimise Your Delivery**

Finally, delivering your message with clarity and confidence is essential. The V·O·I·C·E framework emphasizes the importance of variety in your tone and presentation style. Use modulation, adjust your pitch, and maintain strong body language to convey both authority and approach-ability. Varying your tone of voice and delivery keeps the presentation dynamic and prevents monotony, while also highlighting key points and emphasizing emotion where necessary.

In addition to tone, make sure your message is clear and articulate. Avoid jargon or overly complex language that could confuse your audience. The goal is for them to follow along easily and retain the core message.

Incorporating these best practices into your presentation not only helps you connect more effectively with your audience but also ensures that your message is impactful, memorable, and actionable.

Leveraging the V·O·I·C·E for Engagement Launchpad carries significant financial implications for an organisation, both in tangible and intangible ways. By mastering the art of impactful presentations, HR professionals can drive business success, not just by enhancing communication but by directly influencing the organization's bottom line.

On the tangible side, the financial benefits are clear and measurable. HR professionals who become adept at delivering engaging and persuasive presentations are better positioned to secure buy-in from stakeholders, leading to quicker decision-making and smoother implementation of key initiatives. For example, when HR professionals present employee engagement programs or new HR technologies effectively, they reduce the likelihood of resistance and misunderstandings. This accelerates the adoption process, allowing the organisation to benefit from these programs more swiftly, which, in turn, improves productivity and operational efficiency. The faster projects are completed, the quicker the business can experience cost savings and potentially increased revenue, whether through more streamlined operations or the introduction of new, innovative solutions that drive profitability.

The V·O·I·C·E framework also empowers HR professionals to negotiate and foster partnerships more effectively. Confident communication is key to building strong relationships with external stakeholders, vendors, and even internal departments. By mastering public speaking and storytelling, HR professionals are better equipped to secure resources, negotiate favourable contracts, and collaborate on initiatives that ultimately benefit the entire organisation. Whether it's gaining additional budget for key HR projects or negotiating better deals with suppliers, the ability to communicate persuasively can result in tangible financial benefits that enhance the department's and, by extension, the company's overall financial health.

However, the intangible financial implications are equally critical, even though they may be harder to measure. A confident, engaging HR professional enhances the overall credibility and trust in the HR department. When leadership and employees trust HR, it creates a ripple effect throughout the organization, improving internal relations and boosting employee satisfaction. When employees feel valued and inspired by their leaders, they tend to be more engaged and motivated, which reduces absenteeism and enhances productivity. An engaged employee base is more likely to collaborate effectively, innovate, and contribute to a positive work culture. All these factors lead to a more cohesive workplace, where employees are aligned with the company's goals and are committed to its success.

Over time, this intangible benefit of trust and engagement can significantly enhance an organisation's reputation, both internally and externally. Internally, the HR department becomes a key driver of cultural transformation, making the company more resilient and adaptable to change. Externally, the company's reputation as a great place to work can attract top talent and improve relationships with customers and partners. As more businesses recognise the importance of a strong employer brand, the ability to retain top talent and foster loyalty among employees becomes a competitive advantage that directly impacts long-term financial performance.

The financial implications of mastering the V·O·I·C·E for Engagement framework go far beyond the immediate impact of delivering a great presentation. Tangibly, it leads to cost savings, higher productivity, reduced turnover, and improved operational efficiency. Intangibly, it builds a stronger, more cohesive workforce, enhances trust in HR, and boosts the company's overall reputation. Together, these factors create a cycle of growth, innovation, and profitability, which not only benefits the HR department but also contributes to the organization's long-term success.

When it comes to creating powerful and engaging presentations, especially in HR, it's essential to recognise that you're not just delivering information but you're aiming to shift beliefs, influence decision-making, and drive action. The beliefs and thinking of your audience are pivotal, as they shape how they feel and react. To navigate this effectively, it's important to guide your audience through these mental shifts subtly, often without them realising it.

One of the best ways to achieve this is by crafting your message with stories, analogies, and visuals that resonate with their values and experiences. Stories engage the mind emotionally, making it easier for your audience to connect with your message and start thinking differently. They relate to the characters, challenges, and outcomes in your narrative, often aligning the story with their own personal or business experiences. By doing so, you ease them into new perspectives without triggering defensiveness or resistance. So here is a workplace example:

Anna, an HR manager, had to announce changes to the company's benefits package. She used **intonation** to deliver the message effectively to the staff. She started with a warm tone, acknowledging concerns: "Good morning, everyone. I know that changes like these can sometimes be concerning, and I want to assure you that we've carefully considered what's best for all of us." She then used enthusiasm to highlight improvements: "We're thrilled to announce that we're expanding our healthcare coverage to include more services at no additional cost to you!" When discussing cuts, her tone was clear and steady: "However, to balance these enhancements, we've had to make some adjustments to our vacation policy. This wasn't an easy decision, but it's necessary for the sustainability of our benefits program." Finally, she reassured employees with a confident tone: "We're committed to supporting you through these changes and are here to answer any questions you might have." This approach by Anna helped maintain morale and trust.

Intonation ultimately adds an element of life and humanness to our interactions. These foster trust in the workplace between HR personnel and staff. Without effective intonation, Lilly's message about changes to the benefits package could have resulted in increased anxiety, loss of engagement, miscommunication, decreased morale, and erosion of trust. A monotonous delivery might have made employees anxious, disengaged, and confused about the details of the next steps. Key points could have been overlooked, leading to misunderstanding. Without enthusiasm and reassurance, which lies the HR professional's tone of voice, employees might have felt unsupported, leading to a loss of trust in the company's leadership. Effective intonation helps convey emotions, clarify messages, and build a stronger connection with the audience, which is essential when presenting anything as an HR Manager.

An example **of ensuring you provide clarity and action steps**

Luke, the HR Manager, presented a new remote work policy using clear takeaways and action steps. He included in his presentation to the company that all full-time employees with at least six months of tenure were entitled to work remotely, maintaining regular work hours from 9 am to 5 pm and ensuring regular check-ins with their teams and managers. He then asked all employees to review the policy document that he emailed to them, set up a dedicated workspace at home with reliable internet, and attend a virtual Q&A session on Friday at 10:00 for further feedback and questions. Lukes's approach ensured that all employees were given an opportunity to understand the new policy and know what actions to take, fostering a smooth transition to remote work and adjustment to the new policy. Further, he ensured that all details regarding the new policy were presented in a clear and concise manner to the employees, with the next step being clearly relayed, so that all staff were made aware that they were required to attend a further Q&A session on Friday.

Another key point is the emotional state of your audience. People's decisions are heavily influenced by their emotions, and your presentation should be designed to evoke the right feelings at the right times. For example, if your aim is to encourage action, provide a clear, step-by-step roadmap that outlines the changes they need to make, along with the benefits of each step. Breaking down large tasks into smaller, manageable steps makes the process feel less overwhelming and builds confidence in their ability to act.

HR professionals can often encounter resistance when proposing new initiatives or changes, especially when business leaders are comfortable with the status quo. However, by presenting your ideas in a way that naturally aligns with the audience's current beliefs and values and gently guiding them to see the benefits of change you increase the likelihood that they will not only accept the new ideas but champion them. This can shift your client's mindset from a pattern of resistance (fear of change, procrastination) to a pattern of gain, where they feel empowered to make proactive decisions.

Presenting in this way isn't just about delivering facts; it's about guiding your audience through a process of self-realization and helping them understand that embracing change will ultimately lead to better results. By trusting the process and investing in developing these presentation skills, HR professionals can significantly enhance their impact, influence leadership decisions, and drive the business forward.

Therefore, **master the art of presenting,** particularly by using tools like storytelling, and emotional engagement. This can help HR professionals shift beliefs, influence decision-making, and foster action. By subtly guiding your audience through these shifts, you can reduce resistance, increase buy-in, and pave the way for more impactful HR initiatives. This skill is essential for influencing leaders to embrace the changes necessary to drive organizational success.

The tangible benefits can be measured in terms of cost savings and increased revenue, while the intangible benefits are more about creating long-term value, improving reputation, and fostering a more cohesive workplace.

On the tangible side, HR professionals who master the art of delivering impactful presentations with the V·O·I·C·E for Engagement framework are likely to close more deals and gain buy-in for key initiatives more easily. Presenting HR solutions in a compelling way helps the organisation save time and money by reducing resistance from stakeholders, improving decision-making speed, and eliminating misunderstandings. For instance, effectively communicating the benefits of employee engagement programs or new HR technologies can lead to faster implementation, increasing productivity, and lowering employee turnover rates. All these lead to financial gains by optimising operational efficiency and cutting down recruitment and onboarding costs.

Additionally, an HR professional who is confident in public speaking and storytelling is better equipped to negotiate, foster partnerships, and secure resources for their department, which directly translates into financial benefits for the business. This is especially important when trying to position HR as a critical business driver that contributes to profitability and overall organizational success.

The intangible financial implications are just as powerful, although harder to measure directly. A confident and engaging HR professional enhances the credibility and trust placed in HR. This perception can improve internal relations, increase employee satisfaction, and enhance company culture. When employees feel valued and inspired by leadership, they are more likely to stay engaged and motivated, reducing absenteeism and improving productivity across the board. This is crucial for fostering a positive work environment where people feel invested in the company's success, resulting in long-term loyalty and decreased turnover.

The ability to present HR strategies clearly and compellingly helps in building strong relationships with senior leaders, increasing the chances that HR initiatives will align with broader business goals. This alignment can contribute to better financial performance in the long run, as HR's role in shaping a motivated workforce becomes evident. When it comes to presenting for powerful engagement, HR professionals can make a lasting impact by using a few best practices that help them connect with their audience and deliver their message effectively. The V·O·I·C·E for Engagement is a valuable tool for HR professionals when presenting. Let's take a moment to check these practices for the HR Professional.

Before stepping into any presentation, define your audience. Are you presenting to senior leadership, employees, or external clients? Tailor your content and tone based on their needs, expectations, and level of knowledge. The more relevant your message is to your audience, the more engaged they will be. For example, focusing on how HR initiatives drive business growth will resonate more with executives, while discussing employee engagement strategies might be more appropriate for staff meetings.

A great presentation is rooted in storytelling. People are more likely to engage with and remember a narrative than a list of facts and figures. Weave your key points into a story that outlines the challenges, solutions, and benefits of your HR strategies. For example, share a success story of how a particular HR intervention positively impacted employee morale or retention. By grounding your data in real-life examples, you make your message more relatable and memorable.

Encourage interaction throughout your presentation. Ask questions, invite feedback, or pose scenarios for discussion. When the audience feels like they are part of the conversation, they are more likely to stay engaged and retain the information. This back-and-forth also provides valuable insights into how well your message is resonating and allows you to adjust your approach in real time if needed.

Every great presentation ends with a clear takeaway or action step. Summarise your key points and let your audience know what they can do next, whether it's implementing a new HR strategy, adopting a new mindset, or following up on a particular initiative. A strong call to action helps ensure that your message continues to have an impact after the presentation is over.

In conclusion, leveraging the V·O·I·C·E for Engagement through The Personal Power V·O·I·C·E Launchpad is a critical step for HR professionals looking to elevate their presentations and make a lasting impact. This approach allows HR professionals to confidently present their ideas in a powerful and stress-free manner, ensuring that their message resonates with their audience. By focusing on these steps HR professionals can craft compelling presentations that captivate their audience and clearly demonstrate the value of HR initiatives or interventions.

The tangible financial benefits of mastering this presentation system are evident in the form of time savings, increased revenue, and optimised efficiency. By effectively communicating HR strategies, professionals can foster buy-in from stakeholders, reduce employee turnover, and enhance productivity which will ultimately lead to cost savings and greater profitability for the business. Additionally, the intangible benefits, such as enhanced credibility, improved workplace culture, and stronger internal relationships, are equally impactful in driving long-term business success.

By adopting these best practices for presenting with the V·O·I·C·E for Engagement, HR professionals not only position themselves as strategic business partners but also showcase their ability to drive meaningful change within the organisation. Through clear storytelling, audience engagement, and actionable takeaways, HR professionals can 'Enspire' confidence and ensure their efforts translate into real, measurable business outcomes.

"Be a Presence on the Platform and Perform at your Peak Always"

Chapter Five

Promote And Elevate HR through Advanced HR Practices

Promoting HR is like giving your organisation a turbo boost, as a strong people brand supports the organisation's reputation during challenging times.

Well-promoted HR initiatives influence the organisation's reputation as an employer. If done effectively through great HR practice, it attracts diverse, talented individuals and boosts the companies' competitive advantage even more. During challenging times, when the going gets tough, your exceptional HR strategies continue to shine by keeping everyone ahead of the curve.

> **20**
>
> **A strong people brand supports the organisation's reputation during challenging times.**

Promoting HR will also therefore enhance employer branding, meaning that human resources shapes how everyone sees you an organisation as an employer, making you the magnet for top talent. It will also differentiate the human resources services that are being offered and therefore strengthen relationships with clients. It will also better support internal functions and foster innovation. As innovation is not only about now, but also about the 'next big thing' as the HR Landscape is ever changing, ever evolving and always keeping people on their toes.

It's important for Human Resources departments and divisions to continue to promote their unique employee programs and benefits to differentiate the organisation in the market. When you promote your unique HR perks and programs? That's your way of saying, **"We are the place to be"**.

So, to foster a more dynamic organisation culture, human resources needs to promote itself through continuous improvement in employee engagement, development and employee experiences. This means that the way you position the HR value proposition remains paramount, as it also gives you the opportunity to demonstrate Return on Investment (ROI) and the impact to the company's bottom line.

The objective of promoting HR through a strategic partnership and a growth game plan is to equip HR professionals with the skills to Partner, Pitch, Practice and Perform. The tools and techniques to be successful at these skills are to diagnose, demonstrate and deliver value to the company through effective HR Practices.

So, The Advanced HR Practices Growth Accelerator System ™© is a powerful system, which links to a gameplan that emphasises collaboration, skill-building, and execution in a way that leads to success for everyone involved. The framework references where you are now and where you would like to be and what it is that you will do to get there.

The 5 key elements are:

1. Partner: Achieve Goals Through Collaboration

At the heart of the **Gameplan** is the idea of partnering. No one achieves success in isolation, and working together can exponentially increase the chances of reaching shared goals. When you focus on building strong partnerships, you open yourself up to collective wisdom, shared resources, and diverse ideas that push the entire group forward. By partnering effectively, you create synergy, where the outcome is greater than the sum of individual efforts. This collaborative mindset is essential, especially in today's interconnected world, where cross-functional teamwork is often the key to innovation and success. To **Partner** for success, it's crucial for Human Resources professionals to see employees, managers and leaders as internal clients because it sets the stage for a supportive and engaging workplace and ultimately results in successful partnering. Where HR has a great service focus makes HR responsive to their client needs and concerns and as such, they treat their employees as valued clients.

When employees feel respected and cared for it boosts morale and makes work more enjoyable and therefore gives an uplifting overall **engagement boost** to everyone. Through proper partnering even to the individual level **retention magnetism** is created as happy employees stay longer and helps the organisation to retain top talent. HR professionals are also **culture crafters** as they shape the workplace culture and valuing their internal clients promotes a positive and collaborative atmosphere. HR professionals are to create feedback fuel! Through open communication with internal clients as this fuels improvements in HR practices and policies. So ultimately, we partner for **Business Brilliance** as happy and engaged employees drive business success and competitiveness. When HR sees employees as internal clients, in a nutshell, everyone wins, it's a win-win for the organisation and its people.

2. Provide: Offer Value to Others

The next step in the **Gameplan** is about providing value by focussing on and understanding the needs of others and addressing their challenges by offering reliable and actionable solutions. This involves identifying what others need and being proactive in offering it, whether that's knowledge, resources, or support. In a professional setting, providing value might mean sharing expertise with your team or offering mentorship to colleagues. In any context, when you give people what they need to succeed, you become an indispensable part of the equation. This approach also nurtures trust and builds credibility, which are essential components for long-term success. So, go ahead and **'enspire'** those you work with and lead.

3. Promote & Pitch: Present Your Ideas Persuasively

Pitching is your opportunity to showcase your ideas or solutions in a way that resonates with others. A well-crafted pitch is not just about listing facts; it's about telling a compelling story that connects with your audience on an emotional and logical level. Whether you're pitching a new project to your team, selling a product, or presenting a solution to a client, the goal is to inspire confidence and get buy-in. By mastering the art of pitching, you can influence decisions and align others with your vision, helping to drive the initiative forward.

4. Practice: Sharpening Your Skills for Success

Practice is the element that ensures you're constantly improving. Whether it's honing technical skills, improving communication, or refining a process, practicing is about putting in the effort to be better prepared for the opportunities that come your way. The more you practice, the more confident and competent you become, which positions you to take full advantage of those key moments when success is within reach. It's therefore the repetition and commitment to growth that ensures you're ready to perform when it matters most·as an HR Professional. This therefore enhances the growth of the HR professional offering. **So, practice, practice, practice.**

5. Perform: Follow Through and Deliver Results

The final piece of the **Advanced HR Practices Growth Accelerator System ™©** is to perform. This is where everything comes together. You've partnered, provided value, pitched your ideas, and practiced and honed in on your skills, now it's time to deliver on your promises and **produce results.** Performing is about executing your plan, staying focused on your goals, and following through with consistency. By delivering results, you demonstrate reliability and build a track record of success, which not only benefits your current interventions but also paves the way for future opportunities. HR can create a **performance power-up!** by prioritising their internal clients and creating an environment where everyone can thrive and perform at their best for a greater employee experience and client experience.

Each of these elements- **Partner, Provide, Pitch, Practice, and Perform,** plays a critical role in achieving success. Together, they form a dynamic approach that turns collaboration, preparation, and execution into tangible, measurable growth. Whether you're navigating a corporate setting, leading a team, or aiming for business growth, especially to enhance the company's bottom line, this approach is essential for success in any endeavour.

21

Promoting HR also creates a continuous learning environment where HR professionals also learn to navigate and adapt more easily

---

So, promoting HR also contributes to organisational success and competitiveness, as employee engagement and retention promotes employee satisfaction, reducing turnover and maintains productivity. When your people are happier, they stick around for longer and bring their A-game every day.

There are several challenges which HR professionals must face and overcome to deliver on their gameplan. Some common ones that may be encountered and addressed through simplified solutions are in:

Talent Acquisition and Retention: The **Challenge that may arise is finding and** keeping top talent in a competitive market. A recommended **solution is** enhancing employer branding through engaging job postings, showcasing company culture on social media, and offering attractive perks and benefits. Another solution would be to implement a structured onboarding process to integrate new hires smoothly, as this is one of the key employee touchpoints.

On **Employee Engagement and Morale:** the great **Challenge here is** keeping employees motivated and satisfied. A proposed **solution is to** conduct regular surveys to gauge employee satisfaction and engagement levels. and to correlate these outcomes to the customer survey outcomes. Also to implement recognition programs, provide opportunities for career development, and encourage open communication and feedback. Most importantly it's to create great employee experiences through each of the employee touchpoints in the Employee life cycle and offering superior HR engagement practices.

Another challenge relates to **Performance Management**, where you need to ensure fair and effective performance evaluations. A possible **solution:** Train managers on giving constructive feedback and setting SMART (Specific, Measurable, Achievable, Relevant, Time-bound) goals. Use performance management software to track progress and provide ongoing support. To move towards implementing more modern performance management trends effectively, HR can adopt the strategies of:

- **Continuous Feedback & Check-ins,** where the action is to:

  - Replace annual reviews with regular one-on-one check-ins (monthly or quarterly).
  - Use structured discussions to provide real-time feedback and address challenges.
  - Encourage managers to have ongoing coaching conversations rather than one-time evaluations. And the tools that could be used are:
    - Performance management platforms (e.g., Lattice, 15Five, Culture Amp).
    - Slack or Microsoft Teams for quick feedback loops.

- **Focusing on Skills Development & Growth** where the action is to:

  - Implement Individual Development Plans (IDPs) to align employee growth with company objectives.
  - Invest in upskilling and reskilling initiatives through e-learning platforms.

- Reward progress on learning new skills rather than just past performance and tools that used are:

  o LinkedIn Learning, Coursera, or Udemy for skill development.

  o AI-driven learning platforms for personalized training suggestions.

- **Move Towards Team-Based Evaluations** where the action is to:

  - Balance individual and team performance metrics to encourage collaboration.

  - Use 360-degree feedback to incorporate insights from peers, managers, and subordinates.

  - Recognise and reward teams who **demonstrate leadership and collaboration skills**, even if they are not in managerial roles.

- **Leverage AI & Data-Driven Insights,** where the action is to

  - Use HR analytics to track **engagement levels, productivity trends and levels, and skill gaps.**

  - Implement **predictive analytics** to identify employees who may be at risk of disengagement or attrition.

  - Personalise learning and development plans based on **individual strengths and growth areas.**

- **Create a Growth & Development-Focused Culture,** where the action is to

  - Encourage **employee-driven performance management,** where individuals set personal and professional goals.
  - Replace **"performance improvement plans"** with **"growth action plans"** to focus on development instead of punishment.
  - Offer **mentorship, coaching, and upskilling opportunities** to ensure employees feel invested in.

- **Modernise Performance Review Methods,** where the action is to:

  - Use **360-degree feedback** where employees receive input from peers, managers, and subordinates.
  - Implement **self-assessments** where employees reflect on their achievements and challenges.
  - Transition from **formal, rigid appraisals** to **conversational and goal-oriented discussions**

Compliance and Legal Issues also can come with challenges such as staying up to date with labour laws and regulations. A **solution** here would be to conduct regular audits to ensure compliance. Partner with legal experts for advice on complex issues. Provide training to managers and employees on relevant laws and policy updates.

On Managing Organisational Change, the challenge may be guiding employees through transitions like mergers, acquisitions, or restructuring. So, the **Solution is to** communicate the rationale for the changes from the outset, communicate openly about changes, address concerns proactively, and involve employees in the process where possible. Offer support through training, coaching, and reassurance. The rationale for change and transparency through the process are key.

On Workplace Diversity and Inclusion, the challenge is Promoting diversity and creating an inclusive environment. So, the solution is to provide diversity training for employees and managers that fosters a culture where different perspectives are valued and that looks to a programme that is acceptable to all and builds this capability across the organisation. It's important to create an understanding that all people are interdependent and need to connect in order to thrive. Companies that prioritise diversity and inclusion often report on the success of their initiatives by tracking key performance metrics.

These metrics may include representation statistics; however, it's important to ensure that DEI initiatives foster connection. Instead of creating metrics that may unintentionally lead to disengagement, focus on an **appreciative approach** that brings people together and helps them understand their role in achieving strategic objectives. Additionally, assessing and developing cultural intelligence is essential to ensuring that DEI efforts are intentional, purposeful, and focused on building capability while fostering the right advocacy, especially among leadership and across all levels of the organisation.

When it comes to Technology Integration, the **challenge is** adopting and integrating HR technology effectively. And the **solution** is to invest in user-friendly HR software for tasks like payroll, performance management, and employee data management. Always provide training to ensure employees are comfortable using new technologies.

Where you have Budget Constraints the Challenge is Operating within this limited HR budgets. So, the **solution** is to prioritise initiatives that provide the most value to the organisation. Seek cost-effective solutions by leveraging free or low-cost training and development resources. Additionally, consider partnering with businesses to implement targeted interventions where they are most needed for maximum impact to better assist where there may be HR budget constraints.

Employee Wellbeing: Mental: Stress Management

Employee well-being, particularly around mental health and stress management is a growing challenge for HR professionals. The pressures of the modern workplace tight deadlines, high expectations, and the constant need to adapt can lead to significant stress for employees. HR professionals themselves are not immune to this. They often face the dual responsibility of managing their own stress while also creating policies and practices that support the mental well-being of the wider workforce. To manage this, HR professionals must foster a culture of openness where mental health discussions are normalised, and employees feel safe to express their concerns. Implementing stress management programs, offering flexible work arrangements, and encouraging regular breaks or mindfulness practices can go a long way in reducing workplace stress. Additionally, HR can play a pivotal role in providing access to counselling services or Employee Assistance Programs (EAPs), helping employees build resilience in the face of stress. Prioritising mental health in this way not only enhances individual well-being but also boosts overall productivity and morale across the organization.

Some other simplified solutions for HR challenges are in:

- **Communication:** Keep lines of communication open with employees to understand their needs and concerns.
  Some tips to improve communication include:
    o Consider appointing a dedicated resource responsible for internal HR communication from the communication team

- Training and Development: Offer continuous learning opportunities to enhance skills and knowledge.
- Automation: Use of technology for repetitive tasks to free up time for strategic initiatives.
- Feedback Mechanisms: Implement regular feedback loops to gather insights and improve processes.
- Collaboration: Foster collaboration between HR and other departments to align goals and strategies.
- Digitisation: Capitalise on the use of AI, keep abreast of how HR can leverage this to its best advantage.
- The Use of HR Tools such as the Practice Notes, for ease of reference and execution. bitly/hrtools.com

By proactively addressing these challenges and applying a practical approach to solution development, HR professionals can drive organisational success while fostering a positive and engaging work environment for employees.

There are several techniques and tools that can be used to diagnose and address some challenges that may arise. The key skill for HR Professionals to develop and use is diagnosing the customer's need, facilitating the design of the intervention based on that need, and then supporting the client in delivering or deploying an intervention/solution to address the challenge. These include conducting employee surveys, analysing data such as turnover rates, and consulting with department heads. While using these techniques, it is important for HR professionals to identify areas of improvement and alignment with company objectives through effective **diagnosis, design and delivery of the solution.**

To be effective in your **diagnosis** you need to **develop key strategic partnerships** within the organisation emphasising collaboration with key leaders and stakeholders, such as department heads, executives and employees. Effective strategies for building strong partnerships include clear communication, active listening, and mutual goal setting. Additionally, clarifying expectations and dedicating time to assess and align on necessary interventions, particularly those with a broad company-wide impact, ensures meaningful collaboration and successful implementation. Some great successful collaborations would be developing a sales team incentive programme or working with operations to develop an agreed service level agreement on delivery of all HR responsibilities. Implementing strategies to build trust in the context of championing great employee engagement and experiences requires a thoughtful and consistent approach.

To be effective in your **diagnosis** you need to **develop key strategic partnerships** within the organisation emphasising collaboration with key leaders and stakeholders, such as department heads, executives and employees. Strategies to build strong partnerships are effective communication, active listening, and mutual goal setting. and clarifying expectations and ensuring that dedicated time is set aside to confirm what interventions need to be implemented especially those that would have an overall wide company impact. So, for example, turnaround times in reverting to an intervention or HR programme that needs to be delivered even at the smallest level, that being an administrative task. Some great successful collaborations would be developing a sales team incentive programme or working with operations to develop an agreed service level agreement on delivery of all HR responsibilities.

Here's how you can put these strategies into practice:

- **Transparent Communication:** Foster openness and honesty in communicating company goals and decisions.

    o Hold regular meetings and town halls to share company updates, challenges, and strategic goals.

    o Use multiple communication channels (email, newsletters, intranet) to ensure information reaches all employees.

o Encourage two-way communication by soliciting feedback and addressing questions openly.

- **Consistency:** Demonstrate reliability and integrity by following through on commitments.

    o Set clear expectations and goals for projects, roles, and responsibilities.
    o Follow through on commitments and deadlines consistently.
    o Ensure policies and procedures are applied fairly and consistently across all levels of the organisation.

- **Empowerment:** Involve employees in decision-making and delegate responsibilities to show trust in their abilities

    o Set clear expectations and goals for projects, roles, and responsibilities.
    o Follow through on commitments and deadlines consistently.
    o Ensure policies and procedures are applied fairly and consistently across all levels of the organisation.
    o Delegate decision-making authority to teams and individuals where appropriate.
    o Provide autonomy in how tasks are accomplished, allowing employees to use their skills and creativity.

- Support employee initiatives and ideas that contribute to organisational goals.

- **Recognition and Appreciation:** Regularly acknowledge and celebrate employees' contributions and achievements.

  - Establish formal and informal recognition programs to celebrate achievements and milestones.
  - Personalise recognition efforts to match individual preferences (e.g., public acknowledgment, private praise).
  - Ensure recognition is timely and specific, linking it directly to behaviours or outcomes that align with company values.

- **Fairness:** Ensure fairness in policies, procedures, and interactions with employees

  - Review and update policies regularly to ensure they are fair and equitable.
  - Address conflicts or issues promptly and impartially, using a transparent process.
  - Train managers and leaders on bias awareness and inclusive practices to promote a culture of fairness.

- **Professional Development:** Invest in employees' growth through training and development opportunities.

- Offer training opportunities that align with employees' career aspirations and organisational needs.
- Provide mentorship programs and coaching to support ongoing learning and skill development.
- Encourage employees to pursue certifications or further education relevant to their roles.

- **Collaboration:** Encourage teamwork and recognise collaborative efforts among employees

  - Foster cross-functional teams and projects to promote collaboration across departments.
  - Create shared goals and objectives that encourage teamwork and collective problem-solving.
  - Recognise and reward collaborative efforts that lead to successful outcomes.

- **Feedback Mechanisms:** Establish channels for feedback to address concerns and improve organisational practices.

  - Implement regular employee surveys, suggestion boxes, or anonymous feedback channels to gather input.
  - Act on feedback by making necessary improvements and communicating outcomes to employees.

- o Encourage open dialogue between managers and employees during performance reviews and check-ins.

- **Flexibility and Support:** Offer flexibility in work arrangements and provide support during challenging times.

  - o Offer flexible work arrangements, such as remote work options or flexible hours, to accommodate diverse needs.
  - o Provide resources and support for employees facing personal challenges or professional development hurdles.
  - o Demonstrate empathy and understanding in times of crisis or significant organisational change.

- **Lead by Example:** Model trustworthy behaviour and ethical leadership to inspire trust throughout the organisation.

  - o Model integrity, ethical behaviour, and trustworthiness in all interactions and decisions.
  - o Communicate openly and **authentically,** demonstrating a commitment to organisational values.
  - o Seek feedback from employees on leadership practices and continuously strive to improve.

By consistently applying these practices, HR professionals and organisational leaders can foster a culture of trust, engagement, and positive employee experiences. This approach not only enhances employee satisfaction and retention but also contributes to overall organisational success and growth.

To advance all HR initiatives and to achieve company objectives, it's important that all the key components within the **growth** plan are clear objectives, actionable steps, timelines and metrics for success. So, if the intervention is to improve employee engagement, it needs to include components of diagnosing, developing and delivering.   In a growing company where people are central to its success and agile technology is used to simplify solutions, technology plays a pivotal role in several key aspects:

- **Enhancing Employee Experience:** Technology can streamline HR processes such as onboarding, performance management, and training, making them more efficient and employee friendly. This enhances overall employee experience and satisfaction.
- **Facilitating Collaboration:** Agile technology tools such as project management platforms (e.g., JIRA, Trello) and communication tools (e.g., Slack, Microsoft Teams) foster collaboration among teams, whether they are co-

located or distributed globally. This improves teamwork and collective problem-solving.

- **Supporting Remote Work:** With flexible work arrangements becoming more common, technology enables remote work through cloud-based systems, virtual meeting tools, and secure access to company data. This flexibility helps attract and retain top talent regardless of geographic location.

- **Enabling Data-Driven Decisions:** Technologies for data analytics and business intelligence (e.g., Tableau, Power BI) provide insights into employee engagement, performance metrics, and customer feedback. This data empowers leaders to make informed decisions that drive company growth and improve operational efficiency.

- **Promoting Innovation:** Agile technology methodologies, such as Agile and Scrum, encourage iterative development and rapid prototyping of solutions. This fosters a culture of innovation where ideas can be tested and refined quickly, leading to faster product launches and improvements.

- **Improving Customer Engagement:** As HR has internal customers for the most part,

---

22

Collaboration is enhanced through cross-functional teamwork and transparent communication

---

Customer relationship management (CRM) systems can be developed and automated as tools to leverage data to personalise customer interactions and improve HR service. This enhances internal customer experience and also drives customer satisfaction and loyalty as a whole, driving revenue growth.

- **Ensuring Security and Compliance:** As companies grow, cybersecurity becomes increasingly important. Technology solutions for data security, encryption, and compliance management (e.g., GDPR, HIPAA) help protect sensitive information and mitigate risks, as HR holds personal data of employees.

- **Scaling Operations:** Cloud computing and scalable infrastructure solutions (e.g., AWS, Azure) provide the flexibility to scale operations rapidly response to growth demands. This ensures that IT resources can support increased workload and expanding customer base efficiently.

- **Adapting to Market Changes:** Agile technology allows companies to pivot quickly in response to market changes or competitive pressures. This agility is crucial for maintaining relevance and seizing new opportunities in dynamic business environments.

- *Driving Competitive Advantage:* Ultimately, technology empowers growing companies to differentiate themselves in the market by delivering superior employee experiences, innovative solutions, and exceptional customer service. This competitive advantage contributes to sustainable growth and long-term success of any organisation.

- So, technology therefore serves as an enabler and accelerator in a growing company where people are central to its success. So to champion the implementation of great employee experiences leverage agile technology solutions effectively, to enhance employee engagement, improve operational efficiency, foster innovation, and ultimately drive business growth and competitiveness in their industry.

- Agile technology methodologies offer organisations significant advantages in today's fast-paced business environment. They provide flexibility and adaptability, allowing teams to respond swiftly to changing requirements and market dynamics. This iterative approach fosters faster time-to-market by promoting incremental releases and continuous improvement.

For more impactful engagement and communication with employees and leadership within the organisation, human resources can consider using the following summary of recommended communication tools for HR professionals:

- **Slack:** Real-time messaging and collaboration platform for team communication and project updates.
- Microsoft Teams: Chat, video conferencing, and file sharing within one platform, integrates well with Microsoft Office.
- Zoom: Video conferencing tool for virtual meetings, webinars, and remote interviews.
- Google Workspace: Includes Gmail, Google Drive, Google Meet, and Google Chat for comprehensive communication and collaboration.
- Workplace by Facebook: Combines social media features with business communication tools like groups, chat, and video calls.
- Trello: Project management tool using boards and cards for organizing tasks and team collaboration.
- Mobile messaging and WhatsApp: For sending out group messages, voice or video messages as reminders of key business cycles such as performance management engagements and so on.
- Asana: Task and project management tool with features for assigning tasks, setting deadlines, and team communication.

- *Slido: Audience interaction platform for meetings and events, enables real-time Q&A, polls, and feedback.*
- *HR software with communication features like self-service portals, document management, and notifications. There are a number of these on the market.*

Collaboration is enhanced through cross-functional teamwork and transparent communication, leading to higher productivity and alignment with business goals. Agile also prioritizes customer satisfaction by delivering value through frequent iterations and responsive development cycles. Moreover, it empowers teams with autonomy and accountability, fostering a culture of innovation and continuous learning. By emphasising quality, risk management, and cost efficiency, agile methodologies enable organisations to optimize resources effectively and maintain a competitive edge in delivering high-quality products or services that meet evolving customer needs.

Ultimately, the success of implementing these initiatives hinges on a collaborative approach where HR professionals and business leaders work in unison, leveraging each other's strengths to drive sustainable growth and organisational excellence.

The problem I see is that HR professionals are not always enabled with the tools to come up with the right solutions for the best possible outcome. They are also not always enabled to articulate the goals and objectives of the recommended intervention for buy-in and implementation. This is sometimes due to an overcomplication of the solution or the intervention or lack of adequate budgeting or a lack of seeing the need to invest. HR Professionals are also not always able to demonstrate the value add of the intervention and the positive impact it would have on the company timeously (e.g. writing a business case indicating the ROI of a project) as such HR focuses less on the strategic HR areas that drive value for the company's bottom line, as they are not able to communicate and implement HR's value proposition effectively.

So, the key skill that needs to be mastered relates to how you need to partner to successfully promote the HR offering or best practice solution and develop the skill of writing proper proposals and pitching these demonstrating the ROI, for its implementation and impact. To support the business to facilitate and drive its improved financial results.

The other problem I see is that HR Professionals often do not see the employees and leadership as their clients and the HR solutions recommended are sometimes complex and laborious. At the opposite end the leadership sometimes see the implementation of the interventions as the role of human resources solely. The consequence of these problems is that the desired accountability is not apparent, so no one drives the implementation of interventions at the level and the speed with which they are required to be implemented for business success. This approach not only teaches but also transforms the way both HR and business think as their current thinking may not be conducive to making all parties move forward in an accelerated way.

To better **direct** all HR initiatives and interventions the HR professional requires strong leadership skills so that they can effectively guide and direct the intervention conversations with individuals and teams to facilitate the correct organisational outcomes. Effective directing promotes alignment, collaboration, and performance excellence, driving the organisation toward success. Directing is important because it provides leadership, coordination, and vision, ultimately leading to success and achievement in all endeavours.

So, the HR Professional needs to reference The Advanced HR Practice Growth Accelerator System to promote the creation and implementation of the HR value proposition. These are the unique benefits and advantages that an organisation offers to its employees and demonstrates ROI and the impact to the bottom-line. This system can be likened to the heartbeat of an organisation, where the pulse represents the flow of information and engagement. Just as a healthy heart ensures that oxygen and nutrients circulate effectively to sustain life, a robust people-centric system drives employee engagement and productivity, ultimately leading to a strong return on investment. The rhythm of this heartbeat reflects the organisation's vitality, ensuring that every investment in talent and culture yields tangible benefits and supports overall financial growth of the company.

The HR professional is to **direct** and **deliver** interventions /solutions that are tailored to the needs of the business in a way that is not only compelling, but in a way that brings company results. The Advanced HR Practices Growth Accelerator System ™© can be referenced to succeed at this. So, applying HR practices in modern corporate environments in an innovative way also involves leveraging data analytics, agile human resources practices, personalised learning, and emerging technologies to create a dynamic and thriving workplace culture. By staying ahead of the curve and embracing innovation, Human Resources professionals can effectively support organisational goals and foster a successful workplace culture to drive greater profits.

HR professionals are therefore able to **direct** as they have a clear understanding of the organisation's vision, mission and values and they would also know what the strategic objectives and deliverables are, and they would support the organisation to make informed decisions based on data analysis and determining the strategic priorities effectively.

By cultivating a deep understanding of the unique dynamics and cultures within their organisations, HR Professionals can tailor their leadership approach to resonate with different teams and individuals that fosters and builds trust through transparent communication and consistent follow-through strengthens relationships with employees and stakeholders.

Additionally, HR leaders should stay abreast of the latest industry trends and best practices, incorporating innovative strategies to keep their interventions relevant and impactful. Through continuous learning and development, HR professionals can maintain their effectiveness and inspire confidence in their leadership, ensuring that their directives lead to tangible, positive outcomes for the organisation. The HR Professionals must support and advise the business on the most appropriate intervention to implement based on the diagnosis. HR professionals would be able to identify the specific issues that require intervention, conduct a thorough analysis to understand the root course and determine the skill knowledge or behaviour that needs to improve and advise on the relevant intervention to resolve.

As alluded to earlier in the chapter, a great advanced HR practice has a framework that helps you to understand:

o where you are now in relation to the intervention or challenge and o where it is that you would like to get to and the simplified

o steps you need to take to close the gap.

The outcome of these steps needs to be linked to sound metrics that demonstrate the Return on Investment and its impact to the bottom line.

So, the steps in each of the elements are to diagnose, design, demonstrate and deliver:

Diagnose

- Gather information from the organisational leadership in terms of what their needs are.
- Gather feedback from employees through surveys or interviews on what their needs and organisational experiences are.
- Review organisational performance metrics and data.
- Identify common issues or areas for improvement.
- Prioritise needs based on urgency and impact.
- Discuss findings

Designing HR solutions

- Based on the findings identify the problem and brainstorm potential solutions
- with a small team.

- Develop a prototype or mock-up of the solution. And test it with a small
- user group.
- Gather feedback and adjust based on user input.
- And throughout the process of diagnosing, designing and delivering HR professionals need to be directing HR Initiatives that demonstrate HR's value.

Directing includes the following steps:

- Understanding the company goals and objectives.
- Identifying HR initiatives that align with company goals.
- Setting clear and measurable goals for HR initiatives.
- Gaining leadership support for HR initiatives
- Creating action plans outlining steps, timelines, and responsibilities

Demonstrate Value includes the following steps:

- Defining specific metrics to measure success.
- Regularly tracking progress against these metrics.
- Analysing results to understand the impact.
- Preparing simple reports or presentations summarising findings.
- Communicating results to stakeholders in clear, concise language.

Deliver HR Solutions

- Develop a plan for implementing the solution.
- Communicate the solution to employees and stakeholders.
- Provide training and support as needed.
- Monitor implementation progress and address any issues.
- Evaluate the effectiveness of the solution and make improvements as
  necessary.

These simplified steps provide a practical framework for HR Professionals to follow when they need to develop and deliver HR solutions for the organisation. They are manageable steps that can address the needs and drive positive change.

The Advanced HR Practices Growth Accelerator System ™© therefore empowers the HR professional to diagnose and deliver a compelling intervention simply, in a way that is sustainable and can be implemented and supported by the business. With practice, the more interventions implemented, the more skilled the HR professional becomes. The system used is easily understood by HR and the client, as it's a winning formula in practice.

The introduction of design principles thinking to develop great HR Practices, especially HR challenges and opportunities, is important. These interventions need to be user centred innovative and impactful. The principles of design thinking include empathy, ideation, prototyping and iteration. HR professionals are encouraged to use these principles where there are opportunities to improve the employee experience in at each of the employee touchpoints within the employee life cycle.

Design thinking has been increasingly applied to HR practices by various companies, leading to enhanced employee experiences and improved business outcomes. Here are a few examples:

IBM

IBM utilised design thinking to revamp its HR processes, focusing on enhancing employee experience and satisfaction. They adopted a user-centred approach to redesign their performance management system, incorporating feedback from employees and managers to make it more agile and supportive of continuous feedback and development. This shift helped IBM align employee goals with business objectives more effectively, leading to increased productivity and engagement.

Airbnb

Airbnb applied design thinking principles to reimagine its employee onboarding process. They identified pain points and opportunities for improvement through empathy mapping and journey mapping exercises with new hires. This led to the creation of a more personalised and engaging onboarding experience that aligned with Airbnb's culture and values. As a result, new employees felt more connected to the company from day one, leading to higher retention rates and faster integration into teams.

Intuit

Intuit leveraged design thinking to innovate its performance review process. They shifted from traditional annual reviews to a more continuous feedback model that emphasises coaching and development. Through prototyping and testing different feedback mechanisms, Intuit created a system that promotes ongoing dialogue between managers and employees, resulting in improved performance outcomes and employee satisfaction.

IDEO

IDEO, a renowned design and innovation consultancy, applied design thinking principles to HR practices within their own organisation. They emphasise a human-centred approach to talent management, focusing on understanding employee needs and aspirations through qualitative research and co-design workshops. This approach has enabled IDEO to create a workplace culture that fosters creativity, collaboration, and employee well-being, contributing to their reputation as a top employer in the design industry.

Cisco Systems

Cisco implemented design thinking to enhance their learning and development programmes. They used empathy-based research methods to understand its employees diverse learning preferences and needs of their employees. This led to the creation of personalised learning experiences and digital platforms that cater to individual learning styles and career aspirations. As a result, Cisco employees reported higher engagement with training initiatives and improved skills development, which directly contributed to better business outcomes.

These examples demonstrate how companies across different industries have successfully applied design thinking principles to HR practices, resulting in more engaging employee experiences, enhanced productivity, and improved business performance. By focusing on empathy, iteration, and collaboration, these organisations have been able to design HR initiatives that align with their employees' needs and contribute to a positive workplace culture.

Another great example of an organisational human resources intervention is an **Employee /Leadership Roadshow**.

What do I mean by this? I mean that an Employee/Leadership Roadshow is a powerful HR intervention designed to bridge the gap between employees and leadership while reinforcing the company's commitment to its people.

This initiative brings employees together, fostering meaningful connections and a deeper understanding of the company's mission, values, and offers. It enables HR to showcase what the company provides while also creating a platform for open dialogue. Employees can share their ideas, concerns, and suggestions, promoting authentic communication. This interactive approach demonstrates leadership's commitment to actively listening, understanding employee perspectives, and addressing key challenges.

The roadshow can be conducted in an engaging and informative manner using an appreciative, conversational, and fun approach. Internally, booths can be set up to represent key employee touchpoints, aligning with the company's Employee Value Proposition (EVP). Some aspects can also be delivered through a digital medium, allowing employees to experience and interact with the EVP firsthand. Throughout this process, the core principles of A.C.T.S. are integrated to ensure employees feel valued and heard.

A successful roadshow strengthens trust, enhances employee engagement, and reinforces commitment to continuous workplace improvements. Additionally, it provides HR and leadership with an opportunity to showcase their creativity, leaving employees energized and fostering a sense of belonging.

This approach also serves as a reference point for key HR interventions. It allows HR professionals to diagnose challenges, analyze root causes, and design targeted solutions based on skill, knowledge, or behavioral gaps. These interventions can be customised to address specific workplace concerns and aligned with insights from Employee Pulse or Engagement Surveys.

The Advanced HR Practices Growth Accelerator System ™© also includes an example of the client engagement process and an approach to be undertaken to win. Therefore, The Advanced HR Practices Growth Accelerator System ™© not only provides direct cost savings and operational efficiencies but also helps foster a thriving, motivated workforce that boosts both employee and customer satisfaction. This approach ultimately leads to improved financial outcomes through greater collaboration, higher employee retention, and enhanced productivity, all contributing to a healthier bottom line. Here's a concise summary of tools and platforms that HR professionals can reference for enhancing their employee engagement practices:

- Employee Engagement Surveys: Tools like SurveyMonkey, Google Forms, or Qualtrics for gathering feedback on satisfaction and organizational culture.

- Communication Platforms: Slack, Microsoft Teams, or Workplace by Facebook facilitate real-time communication and collaboration.

- Performance Management Software: BambooHR, Workday, or SAP SuccessFactors for setting goals, conducting reviews, and tracking progress.

- Recognition and Rewards Platforms: Bonus, Kudos, or Kazoo enable employee recognition and morale boosting.

- Learning and Development Platforms: Udemy for Business, LinkedIn Learning, or Cornerstone OnDemand offer courses for skill development.

- Feedback Tools: TinyPulse, Officevibe, or Glint provide mechanisms for continuous employee feedback.

- Wellness Platforms: Virgin Pulse, Wellable, or Fitbit Health Solutions promote employee well-being.

- Social Networks: Yammer or Workplace by Facebook foster community and collaboration among employees.

- HR Analytics Tools: Visier, Tableau, or PeopleInsight offer insights into engagement metrics.

- Employee Assistance Programs (EAPs): Providers like Morneau Shepell or LifeWorks support employee well-being.

These tools assist HR in implementing effective engagement strategies, fostering a positive workplace culture, and ultimately improving organizational performance through enhanced employee satisfaction and retention.

To effectively **Partner, Provide, Practice and Perform** requires a strong Leadership in HR. There are many different leadership skills and competency models and frameworks that exit. What resonates most with me on key leadership qualities and skills from a human resources perspective relate to the importance of a leader's character, vision, communication, and empowerment to be effective in leadership. These competencies help leaders inspire, motivate, and guide individuals and teams towards achieving shared goals and personal and organisational success. HR Leaders can therefore deploy some of these whilst engaging with those that they lead.

The **key leadership qualities** and competencies that are especially important for HR leaders include:

- Integrity: HR leaders must uphold high ethical standards and show integrity in their interactions with employees, management, and external stakeholders.
- Communication: Effective communication is essential for HR leaders to convey policies, procedures, and expectations clearly. They also need strong listening skills to understand employee concerns and provide proper support.

- *Empowerment: HR leaders empower employees by providing opportunities for growth, development, and decision-making within their roles.*

- *Relationship Building: Building positive relationships with employees, managers, and external partners fosters trust and collaboration, which is critical for HR leaders to effectively support the organization.*

- *Problem Solving: HR leaders often deal with complex employee relations issues and organizational challenges. They need strong critical thinking skills to address issues effectively and implement solutions that align with organisational goals.*

- *Servanthood: Leading with a servant leadership mindset allows HR leaders to prioritize the needs of employees and support their development and well-being.*

- *Team Development: HR leaders are responsible for building and developing effective teams within the HR department and across the organisation. They need to understand team dynamics, leverage strengths, and foster a collaborative environment.*

- *Continuous Learning: HR leaders must stay updated with industry trends, best practices, and legal regulations. Continuous learning allows them to adapt their strategies and policies to meet evolving organisational needs.*

These specific ones are particularly critical for HR leaders to effectively manage people, drive organisational success, and create a positive work environment.

Ongoing support, partnership and follow-through with line management by HR is crucial for several reasons:

- *Ensuring Consistency:* Regular support helps maintain consistency in implementing organisational policies, procedures, and practices across different teams and departments. This consistency fosters a cohesive and unified approach to managing employees and achieving business objectives.

- *Clarifying Expectations:* Continuous follow-up allows HR to clarify expectations and provide guidance on complex or evolving issues. This ensures that line managers understand their roles and responsibilities clearly, reducing ambiguity and improving decision-making.

- *Addressing Challenges:* Line managers often face challenges in handling employee issues, performance management, conflict resolution, and compliance with HR policies. Ongoing support helps HR identify and address these challenges promptly, providing necessary resources, training, or coaching to assist managers in overcoming obstacles effectively.

- *Improving Employee Engagement:* Supportive and well-equipped line managers play a significant role in fostering employee engagement and satisfaction. They are instrumental in providing feedback, recognizing achievements, and addressing concerns promptly. By supporting managers in these efforts, HR contributes to a positive work environment that enhances employee morale and productivity.

- *Developing Leadership Skills:* Continuous support and follow-up offer opportunities for professional development and leadership skill enhancement among line managers. HR can provide training sessions, workshops, or mentoring programs to help managers improve their communication, coaching, and team-building abilities.

- *Monitoring Performance:* Regular follow-up allows HR to monitor the performance of line managers in implementing HR strategies and initiatives effectively. It enables HR to assess the impact of their support efforts and adjust as needed to align with organizational goals and objectives.

- *Building Trust and Collaboration:* Effective support and follow-up build trust and collaboration between HR and line management. It demonstrates HR's commitment to supporting managers in achieving departmental and organisational success, fostering a collaborative relationship based on mutual respect and shared goals.

So, ongoing support and follow-up to line management are essential for maintaining consistency, clarifying expectations, addressing challenges, improving employee engagement, developing leadership skills, monitoring performance, and building trust and collaboration within the organisation. By investing in supportive relationships with line managers, HR contributes significantly to overall organisational effectiveness and employee satisfaction.

HR also plays a crucial role in supporting the sales team by ensuring they have the right talent through effective recruitment and hiring processes. HR also provides training and development programs to enhance sales skills and knowledge. They collaborate with sales managers to set performance goals and metrics, and design compensation packages that motivate and reward sales achievement.

HR supports sales enablement with tools and resources, fosters employee engagement and retention, resolves conflicts, ensures compliance with regulations, and strategically aligns HR initiatives with sales strategies to drive organisational success.

Examples of training programs and initiatives that HR might implement to support sales employees:

- Sales Training Programs:
    - Product Knowledge Training: Ensuring sales teams understand the features, benefits, and competitive advantages of products/services.
    - Sales Techniques and Strategies: Training on effective sales methodologies, objection handling, closing techniques, and relationship building.
    - Customer Persona Training: Teaching sales teams how to identify and understand customer personas to tailor their approach and messaging accordingly.
- Professional Development Programs:
    - Leadership Development: Training programs designed to develop leadership skills among sales managers and team leads.
    - Coaching and Mentoring: Pairing experienced sales professionals with newer team members to provide guidance and mentorship.
    - Time Management and Organisation: Training on prioritisation, time management techniques, and organizational skills to optimise productivity.
- Technology and Tools Training:

- CRM Training: Providing comprehensive training on using Customer Relationship Management (CRM) software effectively to track leads, manage pipelines, and enhance customer interactions.
- Sales Automation Tools: Training on tools that automate repetitive tasks, streamline workflows, and improve efficiency in the sales process.

- Soft Skills Development:
  - Communication Skills: Workshops and exercises to improve verbal and written communication skills, including active listening and effective presentation techniques.
  - Negotiation Skills: Training sessions on negotiation tactics, strategies, and best practices for achieving win-win outcomes in sales negotiations.
  - Selling Skills : Undertaken through mentoring sessions and on the job specifically with a focus on closing deals.

- Industry and Market Training:
  - Market Intelligence: Providing insights into industry trends, competitor analysis, and market dynamics to help sales teams adapt their strategies.
  - Regulatory Training: Ensuring sales teams understand and comply with industry regulations, data privacy laws, and ethical standards.

- Customer Service and Relationship Management:
  - Customer Experience Training: Teaching sales teams how to deliver exceptional customer service, handle customer inquiries, and resolve issues promptly.
  - Building Long-Term Relationships: Training on strategies for building and maintaining long-term relationships with clients and stakeholders.
- Cross-Functional Collaboration:
  - Team Building Workshops: Activities and exercises designed to promote teamwork, collaboration, and trust among sales team members and cross-functional teams.
  - Interdepartmental Training: Training sessions that facilitate collaboration between sales, marketing, product development, and customer support teams to align strategies and goals.

These training programs and initiatives are designed to equip sales teams with the knowledge, skills, and tools they need to excel in their roles. It's important for HR professionals to be aware of these so that they are given first priority in delivery to contribute to organisational success and adapt to the evolving demands of the marketplace.

An Example of how HR can advocate for employees and drive business growth :

HR professionals, including Chief People Officers, HR Executives, and HR Business Partners, play a critical role in both advocating for employees and driving business growth.

1. Advocating For Employees:

- Employee Well-being: The HR team recognises that employees are the most valuable asset, and their growth and development directly impact on their performance and job satisfaction. After conducting surveys, feedback sessions, and analyzing exit interviews, HR professionals identify that employees feel they are lacking opportunities for personal and professional growth.

- Action: The HR team, led by the Chief People Officer, advocates for the introduction of a comprehensive employee development program. This includes mentoring, skill-building workshops, leadership training, and career progression pathways. By aligning the program with employee interests and aspirations, HR ensures that employees feel supported, valued, and have a clear roadmap for career growth.

- Impact on Employees: Employees feel heard, supported, and invested in. The development program not only helps them acquire new skills but also gives them a sense of purpose and motivation. This leads to higher employee engagement, improved job satisfaction, and reduced turnover.

2. **Driving Business Growth:**

- *Aligning Talent with Strategic Goals: At the same time, the HR team recognises that business growth is closely tied to having a skilled, motivated workforce. They understand that employee development leads to higher productivity, better performance, and stronger leadership within the company.*

- *Action: HR works closely with the leadership team to ensure that the development program is aligned with business objectives. For example, if the company is focusing on innovation, HR ensures that the program provides employees with opportunities to develop creative problem-solving and strategic thinking skills. They also track employee performance to ensure the program's measurable impact on business goals, such as increased sales, better customer satisfaction, or improved product development.*

- *Impact on Business: By investing in employee development, the company benefits from a skilled workforce capable of meeting strategic business objectives. Employees bring their newly acquired knowledge to work, contributing to increased productivity and innovation.*

Over time, the company experiences business growth in terms of both financial performance and market reputation.

3. **Building a Culture of Advocacy and Growth:**

- *Action: The HR team, especially HR Business Partners, continuously engage with employees, ensuring that the development program is responsive to evolving needs and business demands. They provide consistent feedback loops, hold check-ins with department leaders, and measure the program's impact on employee engagement and business outcomes.*

- *Impact: This ongoing collaboration helps build a culture of continuous improvement where employees feel their career development is integral to the company's success. This mutual respect between employees and the organisation fosters a positive, high-performance culture that drives both employee retention and business profitability.*

Key Takeaways:

- *Advocacy for employees: HR professionals advocate for employee growth by listening to their needs, offering development programs, and supporting their long-term* career goals. This results in a more engaged and satisfied workforce.

- Business growth: By aligning these initiatives with business objectives, HR ensures that employee development drives measurable business results like increased productivity, innovation, and employee retention, which ultimately contribute to business success.

In this example, the HR team bridges the gap between employee needs and organisational goals, creating a win-win scenario where employees thrive and the business flourishes.

A Coaching Summary for a strategic HR Leader and Professional. The person to be coached in this next example is Emma. By coaching Emma through these steps, she is guided to:

1. **Advocate for employee development** by aligning programs with individual career aspirations.

2. **Create a sustainable development program** that drives business growth and improves employee engagement.

3. **Measures success** to ensure the program delivers tangible outcomes, adjusting as necessary to meet both employee and business needs.

Scenario and Background:

Implementing a People-Focused Leadership Development Program to Improve Company Performance based on a Scenario:

*The company, TechX Solutions, a fast-growing technology firm, has been facing a challenge: while employee engagement and satisfaction are relatively high, **leadership development** has been identified as a key gap. Several managers and team leaders have technical skills but struggle with **leadership capabilities** such as team management, conflict resolution, and strategic decision-making.*

This has resulted in inefficiencies, team friction, and stagnated innovation. As a result, the company has seen slowdowns in performance and decreased ability to scale effectively.

*The **Chief People Officer** recognises this as an opportunity to **partner with leadership** and introduces a **people-focused intervention** that can address leadership gaps and ultimately improve company performance.*

As Emma is the coachee she is guided to undertake the following steps:

Step 1: Identifying the Need and Collaborating with Leadership

HR Role: Emma is to sit down with the leadership team, including the CEO, to discuss the company's ongoing challenges and how **leadership development** can improve the organisation's effectiveness.

Coaching Questions for Emma:

o "What specific challenges do you think your managers and team leaders are facing in terms of leadership?"

o "How does the lack of leadership development impact employee productivity and innovation?"

o "What specific outcomes would you like to see from this intervention, and how will you measure success?"

After an open discussion, the leadership team agrees that the lack of strong leadership is contributing to the company's **performance plateaus**, poor **team dynamics**, and slow response to market changes.

HR Action: Emma addresses the outcome of the engagement with the HR team and together they confirm the leadership gap primarily lies in: Emotional Intelligence (EQ), Social Intelligence (SQ) Cultural Intelligence (CI) Conflict Management, and Strategic Thinking.

Emma proposes a leadership development program tailored to address these gaps, aimed at equipping managers with the tools to **inspire, motivate,** and **manage teams** effectively, while aligning their leadership practices with the company's strategic goals.

Step 2: Designing the People-Focused Leadership Development Program

HR Role: Emma works closely with department heads and the leadership team and the HR team to develop a customised leadership development program. The program's goal is to increase leadership competency in the areas of team collaboration, conflict resolution, and strategic decision-making.

Emma's Questions to leadership (Coaching Questions)

- o *"How can we ensure that leadership development aligns with TechX Solutions' long-term goals, such as market expansion and innovation?"*

HR Response to this : The program will be structured as a mix of:

- Workshops on leadership theories, strategic decision-making, and emotional intelligence.
- Interactive scenarios and role-playing to build confidence and skills in conflict management and effective communication.
- Coaching sessions for individual managers to work on specific challenges they face in their teams.

- Mentorship from senior executives for one-on-one leadership guidance and skill refinement.

The program will last for six months, with measurable milestones to track progress and adjust as needed. HR also ensures that the program will include continuous feedback loops, allowing employees and managers to provide input on the training's effectiveness.

Step 3: Gaining Buy-In and Launching the Program

HR Role: HR Team and Emma partner with leadership to communicate the benefits of the leadership development program to all managers and team leaders, ensuring alignment between the program's goals and the broader business strategy.

Communication Strategy:

- HR arranges a company-wide meeting where the CEO and CPO introduce the leadership development program to demonstrate commitment from the top.

- HR explains how the program is designed to empower managers and enhance their ability to lead teams effectively, thereby driving business performance and employee satisfaction.

HR Action: The HR team ensures the program includes:

- Clear messaging about the importance of leadership development for both personal growth and company success.

- Training materials that directly link the program's content to the company's mission, vision, and growth strategy.

Step 4: Implementation and Tracking Progress

HR Role: During the program, **HR Business Partners** work directly with managers and leaders to **monitor progress** and offer ongoing support. They serve as **mentors**, guiding leaders through the program whilst Emma has oversight. The team also ensures that the leadership intervention remains aligned with the company's performance objectives.

Coaching Check-In: HR checks in with department heads regularly to get feedback on how the managers are applying what they've learned. They ask:

  - "How are managers implementing leadership skills within their teams?"

  - "Have you noticed any improvements in team collaboration or productivity?"

- "What challenges are you still facing as a result of leadership gaps?"

HR Action: The HR team also collects data and feedback through:

- **360-degree feedback** from team members about how leadership has improved.

- **Employee satisfaction surveys** focused on team dynamics, communication, and leadership effectiveness.

- **Performance reviews** that assess how leadership capabilities are impacting team productivity and business outcomes.

Step 5: Measuring Success and Adjusting the Program

HR Role: After the program ends, Emma together with the team evaluates the impact of the leadership development program on company performance.

Coaching Check-In:

- "Have we seen measurable changes in leadership effectiveness and team performance?"

- "What business outcomes (e.g., sales growth, employee retention, productivity) have improved as a result of the leadership intervention?"

HR Action: The HR team with Emma analyses data on:

- *Employee engagement and satisfaction scores before and after the program.*

- *Business performance metrics, such as revenue growth, client satisfaction index and employee turnover, comparing them to the program's launch date.*

- *Leadership performance reviews, identifying improvements in decision-making and team leadership.*

Step 6: Continuous Improvement and Scaling

HR Role: With successful outcomes, the CPO and HR Business Partners collaborate with leadership to make leadership development an ongoing part of the company culture, ensuring the program is scaled and refined for future cohorts.

Coaching Action:

- *"How can we ensure that leadership development remains a priority as the company grows?"*

- *"What strategies can we use to scale the program to a larger group of managers or even individual contributors?"*

HR Action: Emma and the broader HR team works with leadership to:

- Expand the program for all managers across the company and offer more advanced leadership tracks for senior leadership.

- Integrate continuous learning into the culture, including mentorship programs and self-paced learning modules to reinforce leadership skills long-term.

Results and Impact on Company Performance:

1. Improved Leadership: Managers demonstrate increased emotional and social intelligence, better decision-making, and more effective team management.

2. Increased Employee Engagement: Teams report higher levels of engagement and productivity as leaders improve communication, foster collaboration, and resolve conflicts more effectively through intentional conscious commitment to activate a great employee experience.

3. Business Performance: There is a measurable improvement in company outcomes, such as revenue growth, client retention, and operational efficiency, driven by stronger leadership.

4. Employee Retention: Managers who are better equipped to lead their teams contribute to reduced turnover and a stronger company culture.

In conclusion, through a strategic partnership between HR professionals and leadership, the company successfully implements a people-focused leadership development program. This collaboration directly addresses leadership gaps, enhances company performance, and fosters a culture of continuous growth and improvement. Emma, as the HR Executive, ensures that the program stays aligned with business goals and delivers tangible results for the organisation.

In conclusion, The Advanced HR Practices Growth Accelerator System ™© equips HR professionals with the essential tools/skills to become dynamic leaders in their organisations. By focusing on key elements like partnering, providing value, pitching ideas, practicing skills, and performing with excellence, and the application of this simplified system HR professionals can effectively diagnose challenges, design solutions, and deliver impactful results. The true power of this system lies in its ability to foster collaboration and build trust among stakeholders. By engaging leadership and employees alike, HR can promote a thriving workplace culture where individuals feel valued and supported. This, in turn, leads to happier employees, more satisfied customers, and long-term profitability. The tangible benefits of cost savings, along with the intangible advantages of a stronger workplace culture, come together to create sustainable growth for the organisation. The Advanced HR Practice Growth Accellerator system also provides both tangible and intangible financial benefits for HR professionals and their companies.

Tangibly, it improves cost-efficiency by streamlining resources, reducing redundancies, and enhancing employee retention, which leads to savings in recruitment and onboarding costs. Intangibly, it boosts the credibility of HR, fosters better workplace culture, and leads to higher employee and customer satisfaction and most importantly the growth of the company.

These improvements result in increased productivity, collaboration, and long-term profitability for the company.

Points to Ponder : in your environment:

- o What current HR practices in your organisation align with this system or framework?
- o Which element of the Advanced HR Practices Growth Accelerator System do you struggle with the most? How can you improve?
- o How does your HR team currently advocate for a great employee experience? What strategies can you implement to enhance this?
- o Can you think of an instance where HR advocacy influenced a major business decision? What was the impact?

So Ultimately, The Advanced HR Practices Growth Accelerator System ™© empowers HR to become trusted executives and strategic partners. By implementing these practices, HR leaders can drive meaningful change, enhance their credibility, and contribute significantly to the overall success of the business.

Through continuous collaboration, skill-building, and a commitment to excellence, HR well-positioned to **Elevate** their HR Practices which in turn helps their organisations thrive in today's competitive landscape.

"When we accelerate great HR Practices, we don't just transform workplaces , we ignite the potential of people to drive extraordinary results"

Chapter Six

Cracking The Code

So, let me take you back to the introduction where I wrapped up by asking you to keep the People to Profit Practice Code ™© in your back pocket. This code is all about the realisation that:

Happier HR Professionals = Happier Employees = Happier Customers = Greater Company Profits

To bridge the gap between employee engagement and customer satisfaction, HR professionals can start by comparing insights from both employee and customer surveys to uncover shared themes like job satisfaction, communication flow, and a positive workplace atmosphere.

By seeing how happy employees often lead to happier customers, they can identify key areas where an engaged workforce improves the overall customer experience. By spotting these trends, HR can figure out where boosting employee morale could level up the customer experience. Plus, collaborating with teams that interact directly with customers helps HR understand how employee attitudes shape those all-important customer moments, leading to smarter training and strategies that make everyone, employees and customers smile.

In correlating the employee experience with the customer experience, it encourages HR Professionals to foster a workplace culture that prioritises employee engagement, satisfaction, and empowerment, as motivated and happy employees are more likely to deliver exceptional service and create positive customer interactions.

To correlate an employee, experience rating with a customer experience rating, HR Professionals would look at the relationship between how employees feel about their work environment and how customers feel about their interactions with the employees in the company.

Several studies have explored the connection between employee experience and customer experience, demonstrating that improvements in employee satisfaction can lead to enhanced customer satisfaction. Here are a few notable ones:

- Gallup's State of the American Workplace Report:

  - Outcome: Gallup's research shows a strong link between employee engagement and customer engagement. Companies with highly engaged employees see 10% higher customer ratings, 20% higher sales, and 21% higher profitability. Engaged employees are more likely to provide better service, which translates to better customer experience.

- Harvard Business Review - "The Employee-Customer Connection":

  - Outcome: This study found that organisations with higher employee satisfaction scores also had better customer satisfaction scores. Specifically, companies in the top quartile of employee satisfaction had a 2.5 times higher likelihood of being in the top quartile of customer satisfaction.

- "Linking Employee Satisfaction to Customer Satisfaction" by Heskett, Sasser, and Schlesinger:

  - Outcome: This classic study, often cited in the field, revealed that employee satisfaction is a leading indicator of customer satisfaction. The researchers found that companies that invest in their employees see better customer service, which improves customer loyalty and satisfaction.

- The "Service Profit Chain" Model by James L. Heskett, W. Earl Sasser Jr., and Leonard A. Schlesinger:

    o Outcome: This model illustrates that employee satisfaction leads to improved service quality, which in turn leads to higher customer satisfaction and increased profitability. The model has been widely validated and is used to emphasise the importance of investing in employee experience to drive customer satisfaction.

- "The Relationship Between Employee Satisfaction and Customer Satisfaction in the Retail Industry" by Anca Toma and Monica Dinu:

    o Outcome: This study highlighted that higher employee satisfaction in the retail sector correlates with improved customer satisfaction scores. Retailers with happier employees tend to have better customer experience, demonstrating the direct impact of employee morale on customer interactions.

- "Impact of Employee Satisfaction on Customer Satisfaction in the Indian Retail Sector" by R. Sharma and M. Talwar:

- Outcome: The research found a positive correlation between employee satisfaction and customer satisfaction in the Indian retail sector. Companies with satisfied employees provided better customer service, which was reflected in higher customer satisfaction scores.

These studies collectively underline the importance of **focusing on employee experience** as a crucial factor in driving positive customer experience and overall business success.

HR Leaders and professionals in companies play a pivotal role in ensuring that employee satisfaction remains high, which in turn enhances service quality, customer satisfaction, and profitability. Here is how they can contribute more effectively:

Foster a Positive Work Environment

- Promote a Healthy Culture: Cultivate a workplace culture that values respect, inclusion, and open communication. This helps employees feel valued and supported.

○ Encourage Work-Life Balance: Implement policies that support work-life balance to reduce burnout and increase job satisfaction.

Employee Development and Engagement

- Training and Development: Offer continuous learning opportunities to help employees grow professionally and personally. This boosts their confidence and performance.
- Recognition Programs: Develop recognition and reward programs that acknowledge and celebrate employee achievements and contributions.

Effective Communication

- Regular Feedback: Facilitate regular feedback sessions to understand employee concerns and address them promptly. This shows employees that their opinions are valued.

- Transparent Communication: Ensure transparent communication regarding company goals, changes, and expectations. This helps employees feel connected to the company's mission.

Career Advancement Opportunities

- *Clear Career Paths:* Provide clear pathways for career progression within the organisation. Employees are more satisfied when they see opportunities for advancement.

- *Mentorship Programs:* Implement mentorship and coaching programs to guide employees in their career development.

Employee Well-being

- *Health and Wellness Programs:* Offer wellness programs that address physical and mental health, such as fitness memberships, counseling services, and stress management workshops.

- *Safe and Supportive Environment:* Ensure a safe work environment and provide support for employees dealing with personal or professional challenges.

Performance Management

- *Fair Evaluation Systems:* Develop fair and consistent performance evaluation systems that provide constructive feedback and set achievable goals.

- *Incentives and Compensation:* Ensure competitive compensation and benefits packages that reflect the value of employees' contributions.

Aligning Employee and Customer Experience

- Customer-Centric Training: Provide training that aligns employee roles with customer expectations and service standards.

- Feedback Loop: Create systems for employees to share customer feedback and insights, helping them understand the impact of their work on customer satisfaction.

Leadership Development

- Supportive Leadership: Train leaders to be supportive and empathetic, as effective leadership directly influences employee morale and engagement.

- Manager Training: Equip managers with skills to effectively manage teams, resolve conflicts, and motivate employees.

Monitoring and Evaluation

- Track Satisfaction Metrics: Regularly measure employee satisfaction through surveys and feedback mechanisms. Analyze the data to identify trends and areas for improvement.

- Adjust Strategies: Use insights from satisfaction metrics to refine HR strategies and interventions.

By applying these strategies, HR professionals can cultivate an environment that boosts employee satisfaction, which in turn leads to improved service quality, higher customer satisfaction, and greater profitability.

> ## 23
>
> ### The People to Profit Practice Code addresses the Happy HR Professional first

The People to Profit HR Practice Code addresses the Happy HR Professional first, so that they are equipped to create a conducive environment where there are happier employees. The People to Profit HR Practice Code empowers HR professionals to understand their own capabilities and enables and equips them to fulfil their responsibilities effectively. This code provides them with the essential skills and tools equip, empower, enables, engages and elevates the HR Professionals by pointing them to the necessary skills needed to enhance employee engagement and experience. It also offers practical resources to help HR professionals demonstrate their contribution and impact to the company's commercial success and overall bottom line. HR professionals can therefore use reflective metrics to showcase their contributions and demonstrate their added value.

In conclusion The People to Profit HR Practice Code ™© recognises that People remain integral to the Business because as Humans, we will always value connection! The People to Profit Practice Code is a reveal of what a Superior HR Practice is in a Nutshell.

Throughout The People to Profit HR Practice Code ™© we have explored the transformative potential of integrating human centric fundamentals and the excitingly enriched practices into the realm of Human Resources. We began by establishing foundational fundamentals through sound **protocols**, ensuring that every HR Professional understands the core values and principles that define the profession. We then delved into the importance of activating superior HR **practices**, highlighting the need for quick and impactful interventions that align with the business objectives and goals, for greater results and impact.

By **positioning** human resources strategically, we demonstrated how a consistent image of growth can drive both employee satisfaction and corporate success through the people to profit pathway. Leveraging the power of the HR voice, we learned how to effectively communicate, engage through **presenting** to employees and all stakeholders, making our HR solutions compelling and inspiring.

Finally, we emphasised the significance of advocating for and promoting great HR practices, through providing practice notes and a framework and method for immediate and impactful implementation through advocating a win and growth plan to **promote** and elevate the work of HR. The journey of an HR professional is one of continuous learning and evolution in a rapidly changing business environment., staying ahead of the curve is what matters. This book also encourages you to stick to the journey and to embrace, ongoing growth and adaptation, not just for yourself but for the entire organisation. By fostering a culture of continuous improvement, you can ensure that your HR practices remain relevant and effective. This involves staying updated with the latest trends and technologies in HR, being open to new ideas and constantly seeking ways to enhance the engagement and employee experience. Remember that growth is not a destination but rather a commitment to your professional journey as the driving force behind your success as an HR Leader and HR Professional.

As this EPIC People to Profit HR Practice Code™© also focuses on **HR Centricity,** and the essence of being human, it gives you the HR EDGE to better deliver your offering so that your clients can also thrive in the workplace. This Code is an approach that can be followed to develop and deliver a simplified, compelling HR solution- from Human Resources Strategy development to the implementation of all the interventions identified within it, which the business welcomes and will be engaged in and with.

By "cracking" The People to Profit Practice Code™ © Human Resources will know and better understand that their success and happiness equals happier employees, happier customers and greater company results and profits! as they are empowered to direct a happier workforce.

The People to Profit Practice Code™©, also assists Human Resources to better guide **Employees and Employers on their journey** to success. It provides the Human Resources professional with some differentiated **"Golden Nuggets" for** improved Human Resource best practices through its people.

As we conclude this journey together, I want to leave a message of inspiration and empowerment, as the role of an HR professional is not just about managing resources but also about nurturing and unleashing the full potential of people.

> **24**
>
> *There is not Growth of Business without the Growth of People*

The message of inspiration is that you have the power and opportunity to transform workplaces, create happier and more vibrant engaged employees to drive significant business outcomes. Embrace this responsibility with passion and dedication, knowing that your efforts can make a profound difference. As you apply the principles and strategies from this book, remember that the essence of great HR practice lies in the genuine compassion and commitment you bring to your work. Stay motivated and inspired and keep learning and continue to push the boundaries of what is possible. Together we can create a future where HR is not just a function but a driving force for growth in every organisation, remembering that there is **no growth of business without the growth of people.**

Golden Nuggets

- *Return to the Essence of Being Human*
- *Increase your self-awareness and the awareness of others around you*
- *Tailor and refine your offering to meet your customers' expectations better!*
- *All thoughts, words and actions of a person need to be aligned so that they can be experienced as authentic and trustworthy*
- *The power of unleashing conscious commitment lies in its ability to drive focus, persistence, achievement, personal growth, trust, resilience, fulfilment and inspiration*
- *As HR professionals we have the power to serve well, all we need is to allow ourselves to claim it, use it and share it!*
- *Elevate our HR practices by leveraging our people through innovative engagement practices, effective communication and cutting-edge technology to dramatically improve the Employee Experience*
- *People need to be at the centre of your HR value proposition*
- *Establishing and providing a superior HR practice contributes to the overall improved management of Human Capital within an organisation*

- *To leverage human capital potential leadership needs to be trained and coached in practice on the people elements that need focus or mastery.*
- *You transform yourself by cultivating an attitude that rethinks, reshapes, reimagine and reclaims your life values and goals*
- *Rebuild a stairwell of small wins to create great employee experiences*
- *Me first, Team first and customer first!*
- *To successfully navigate the people to profit pathway organisations must be equipped with essential principles, innovative strategies and proven best practices*
- *Keep striving & growing & watch your workplace flourish and thrive like never before.*
- *Capture the attention of your audience and you can get their buy in*
- *Always talk about the point before you reveal it*
- *Be a presence on the platform and perform at your peak always!*
- *A Strong people brand supports the organisations reputation during challenging times*
- *Promoting HR also creates a continuous learning environment in which HR Professionals need to navigate and adapt to*

- *Collaboration is enhanced through cross functional teamwork and transparent communication*
- *The People to Profit Practice code addresses the happy HR Professional First*
- *There is no growth of Business without growth of people!*

People to Profit HR Practice Notes : What are these ?

HR Practice notes serve as a valuable resource for HR professionals to ensure consistency, and effectiveness in their work and provides practical guidance on complex or challenging aspects of their profession. The key characteristic of a practice note is that it seeks to provide/offer the following:

1. **Guidance** on how HR professionals should interpret and apply principles in practice.
2. It outlines recommended **best practices** and methodologies that are considered effective or efficient based on industry knowledge and expertise.
3. It may provide **interpretations** to help professionals navigate and comply with requirements.
4. It often includes **examples or case studies** to illustrate how the guidance or best practices can be applied in real-world situations.
5. Practice notes are typically **non-binding**, however, are influential in shaping industry norms and practices.
6. They may be **updated periodically** to reflect changes in, advancements in technology, or evolving best practices.

The practice notes drafted below aim to be a point of reference for HR Professionals before an initiative or intervention is undertaken. The practice notes outlined are the ones that are deemed to be most relevant in creating a great employee experience and may therefore be used in conjunction with what exists in your organisation and can also provide the HR professional with the opportunity to also tailor their intervention depending on the organisational context.

A Generic Practice Note on tackling an HR related challenge or problem: A simplified approach as directed in the Advanced HR Practice Growth Accellerator

1. *Meet with line manager/s.*

2. *Present the approach to be undertaken using Storytelling: Position HR And the advantages of using the approach. The approach is to considers. Where you are now concernign the problem and where you would like to Be once the problem is addressed.*

3. *The Conversation on the problem: (Where are you now?) Problem named, outlined, route course/s of the problem noted and the impact it's having in the area.*

4. *Conversation on where to be once the solutions are implemented. (Where do we need to be?)*

5. *Discuss the steps to get us to where we want to be? (How are we going to get there?)*

6. *Theme name solution and cluster depending on the problem and categorisation of the people that it affects in the area.*

7. *Implementation steps developed with timelines and responsible persons.*

8. *Next Meeting: Progress & Impact of Implementation monitored*

HR Practice Note: Role of Leaders in Leading People

One of a leader's primary role and responsibility is **hiring individuals with diverse skill sets experiences** and perspectives to enrich the organisation.

Leaders are to foster creativity, problem solving and a sense of belonging amongst people. They are as such to ensure that **collaboration and teamwork is encouraged** across functions and divisions.

Leaders need to let their people know and understand the company's vision, and goals, and how their individual contributions contribute to the larger picture. To achieve this communication channels, need to be open and transparent at all levels of the organisation. Empowered employees are more likely to be engaged, curious, innovative, and committed to achieving organisational goals. They take initiative, drive positive change, and contribute to a dynamic and thriving workplace culture.

Provide employees with autonomy to make decisions and take ownership of their work empowers them way beyond many other incentives. Due to the nature of work today it's important to promote a healthy work-life balance to prevent burnout and maintain employee well-being and this can be inclusive of flexible working arrangements, wellness programs and policies that support employees personal and family needs.

Recognise and reward employees for their achievements and contributions and this can be done through monetary incentives and non -monetary rewards such as praise and appreciation programs, promotions and or additional responsibilities.

Investing in the learning and development of employees to enhance their skills knowledge and abilities can be done in a formal and an informal mentorship opportunity.

Implement performance management that provides regular feedback coaching and opportunities for growth for both the individual and the company. This helps employees to understand their strengths and improve their performance which is aligned to the organisational objectives.

Human Resources leadership and professionals must institutionalise business support and collaboration by showing up in all these areas! In summary, the phrase means that HR should actively establish and integrate itself into various aspects of the business by being present and involved in different areas. The goal is to ensure that HR is playing a key role in supporting and fostering collaboration across the organisation. By "showing up" in these areas, HR can build stronger relationships, provide necessary support, and help create a more cohesive and effective work environment. By referencing practical examples within the touchpoints, HR professionals can access a quick point of reference for proven interventions that have been successfully executed.

For instance, during the recruitment touchpoint, using structured interviews and candidate assessment tools can streamline the hiring process and ensure the selection of top talent. In the onboarding phase, a well-designed orientation programme and mentorship initiative can significantly improve new employee integration. Regular performance reviews and feedback sessions during the development touchpoint can help in identifying skill gaps and providing targeted training. Effective use of employee surveys and engagement platforms in the retention touchpoint can foster a positive work environment and address any concerns promptly. These practical examples not only provide peace of mind but also elevate the strategic approach of HR professionals, ensuring they have a solid game plan to enhance their HR practices.HR professionals would have a quick point of reference on proven interventions that have been implemented and worked thus giving them peace of mind and levelling them up in terms of their game plan.

HR Practice Note: Leadership Qualities / Traits that build Strong Teams for leaders: *(A number of studies indicate these percentages)*

1. Be Appreciative: 65% of employees say they are not recognised for the work they do. So, it's important to praise employees when they excel

2. Be Fair: when employees are given a 7 - 9% raise they are inclined to work or motivated to work harder

3. Be Motivating: employees say they would be 20% -60% more productive with great leaders

4. Be Committed; so, employees feel compelled to add value. 13% employees around the world feel Engaged at work.

5. Be Trustworthy: Employees feel comfortable to come to you for advice. 59% of employees leave their organisations, do so due to trust issues

6. Be Organised 69% of employees believe that this is a quality that every strong leader should have.

7. Be a Good Communicator: Open communication is the characteristic they admire most in great leaders

8. Be Positive: being provided with positive feedback is also important A ration of 6:1 positive/negative feedback works best

9. Be Responsive: provide your direct reports with feedback. The way you respond to change and how you

keep staff informed alleviates stress amidst unforeseen circumstances.

10. Be Compassionate: by being introspective and inspiring

HR Practice Note: Developing an Employee Value Proposition

Creating and launching an Employee Value Proposition (EVP) is a strategic process that requires careful planning, clear communication, and execution. The EVP is essentially the unique set of offerings, values, and experiences an organisation provides to its employees. Below are the key steps to create and launch an EVP effectively:

- **Understand the Current Employee Experience**

  - **Conduct Internal Research:** Gather insights through surveys, focus groups, interviews, or feedback sessions with current employees. Understand their motivations, what they value about working for the company, and areas for improvement.

  - **Analyse Exit Interviews:** Review exit interviews to identify common reasons for employee turnover. This can highlight gaps in your current EVP or areas needing improvement.

  - **Evaluate Existing Data:** Look at employee engagement scores, retention rates, and other metrics to understand employee satisfaction and experience.

- **Define the Core Elements of the EVP**

  - *Company Culture:* The EVP should mirror the core values, mission, and culture of the organisation. It must capture the essence of what the company stands for and what makes it unique. So, identify the values, mission, and culture of the organisation that you want to emphasise. **This is the essence of your EVP.**

  - *Compensation and Benefits:* Highlight competitive salary structures, bonuses, stock options, health benefits, retirement plans, and any unique perks (e.g., wellness programs, flexible working). Create an easy to glance at framework with simple explanations

  - *Career Development:* Include opportunities for skill development, training programs, mentorship, and career advancement.

  - *Work-Life Balance:* Showcase flexibility in work arrangements such as remote work options, flexible hours, or paid time off policies.

  - *Recognition and Rewards:* Explain how the company recognises and rewards employees for their contributions.

  - *Job Security:* Reinforce job stability, especially if the organisation has a strong track record of low turnover or a solid growth outlook.

- **Engage Leadership and Key Stakeholders**

  - **Involve Executives:** Ensure that the senior leadership team is on board with the EVP and fully supports its development. Their buy-in is crucial for the initiative's success. Together with them define what the future employee engagement and experiences need to be.

  - **Collaborate with HR:** Work closely with HR to ensure alignment between the EVP and existing policies, processes, and employee benefits.

  - **Cross Department Collaboration:** Engage various departments (e.g., marketing, communications, operations) to gather insights and create a unified approach.

- **Craft the EVP Statement with a Focus on these Key Pillars**

  - **Write a Clear, Concise Memorable Statement:** The EVP statement should be a succinct, compelling summary of what employees can expect from your organisation. It should resonate with both existing employees and potential hires. It therefore requires **Dual Appeal**, with current employees, who want to feel valued and engaged and potential hires, who are considering the company as an employer. It should instantly convey the key benefits of working at the company. It most importantly **needs to be brief, memorable and impactful** - one or two sentences that are easy to understand and remember.

- **Authenticity is key:** Employees and candidates can sense when an EVP is not genuine. Your EVP must be authentic and honestly reflect the actual employee experience. It shouldn't over-promise, idealized portrayals or misrepresent the organization. **Ensure Consistency with Employee Experience so link to Real Experiences:** Ensure that the EVP aligns with what employees experience daily. For instance, if your Employee Value Proposition (EVP) emphasizes collaboration and teamwork, yet employees' express feelings of isolation, there is a discrepancy that requires attention.

- **What Employees Can Expect:** Highlight employee experience in terms of support, recognition, and work-life balance. For example, if your company is known for its supportive environment, inclusion efforts, or emphasis on well-being, include this in the EVP.

- **What You Offer:** Clearly articulate the benefits and advantages of working at your company. This might include competitive pay, career growth opportunities, flexible work arrangements, company culture, job stability, and more.

- **Highlight Differentiators: Show What Sets You Apart:** Identify what makes your company different from competitors in your industry. Whether it's a unique company culture, exceptional career development opportunities, or a strong commitment to diversity, make sure your EVP emphasizes these differentiators.

- **Involve Employees in the Process:** Consider crowd-sourcing input from employees to craft the statement. This ensures it reflects their true experience and helps make the EVP more authentic.

- **Craft an Effective EVP Statement, Be Specific:** Instead of vague statements like "We offer great opportunities," give concrete examples such as "We offer a leadership development program that helps 30% of participants advance to senior roles within two years."

Example of a great statement:

"We empower our employees to grow and succeed by fostering a collaborative and inclusive culture. With,

- o flexible work options,
- o a commitment to professional development, and
- o a competitive benefits package,
- o **we help our people thrive both personally and professionally.**"

- **Test and Improve the EVP**

  - **Pilot with Employees:** Before finalising the EVP, test it with a group of employees across different departments. Gather feedback to ensure the messaging resonates with your audience.

  - **Refine Based on Feedback:** Tweak the EVP based on the feedback received. Make sure it is comprehensive, but not overly complex, and speaks to your target audience's values.

- **Design an Engaging Communication Strategy**

In communication avoid jargon and corporate buzzwords. The language should be straightforward and relatable to employees and potential hires.

  - **Internal Launch:** Announce the EVP internally first, ensuring that employees feel involved and excited about the new proposition. Use company-wide meetings, intranet, and other communication channels.

  - **External Launch:** After gaining internal support, share the EVP externally via your careers page, social media, job advertisements, and recruitment events.

  - **Consistent Messaging:** Ensure that the EVP messaging is consistent across all channels and reinforces the same core values.

- **Integrate the EVP into the Employee Lifecycle**

  - *Onboarding:* Ensure that new hires experience the EVP from day one. Align onboarding materials and activities with your EVP's key messages.

  - *Performance Management:* Align performance management processes with the EVP by incorporating the values and commitments into employee assessments and feedback.

  - *Employee Development:* Make sure career development and training programs reflect the EVP, offering employees clear pathways to growth and advancement.

  - *Retention Strategies:* Utilise the EVP to inform retention efforts. Regularly evaluate whether employees are still experiencing the benefits of your EVP and adjust as necessary.

- **Monitor, Measure, and Adjust**

  - *Track Effectiveness:* Use surveys, interviews, and data analysis to measure how well the EVP is resonating with employees. Track metrics like employee engagement, retention rates, and satisfaction.

  - *Gather Feedback Continuously:* Regularly collect feedback from employees regarding the impact of the EVP on their experience. Are they receiving what was promised in the EVP?

- **Refine the EVP:** Adjust the EVP as needed to ensure it remains aligned with the evolving needs of employees and the organisation. Stay responsive to market trends and shifts in employee expectations.

- **Promote the EVP in Recruitment Efforts**

  - **Attract Talent:** Leverage the EVP to attract new talent by integrating it into recruitment materials, interviews, and job descriptions.

  - **Employer Branding:** Position the EVP as part of your overall employer branding strategy to differentiate your organisation from competitors in the job market.

- **Sustain and Evolve the EVP**

  - **Continuous Communication:** Keep the EVP alive by continuously communicating it within the organisation through employee newsletters, events, and leadership messaging.

  - **Regular Evaluation:** Frequently review the EVP to keep it aligned with evolving employee needs and business changes.

- **Final Checklist in crafting the EVP:**

  - Does it reflect the company's core values?

- Is it authentic and aligned with real employee experiences?
- Is it specific and concise, while highlighting key benefits?
- Does it resonate with both employees and potential hires?
- Does it define what the future employee experience will look and feel like?

By following this streamlined approach, you can create an EVP statement that is clear, authentic, compelling, adaptable, aligned with your organisation's unique offerings and that is impactful. Your EVP can be an effective tool to attract, engage, and retain top talent while aligning employee expectations with the company's mission and goals.

HR Practice Note : The Impact of the Internal Work Environment on Customer Interactions

Here is a straightforward approach that can empowers the HR Professional to better understand the **impact of the internal work environment on customer interactions** and improve both employee and customer experiences simultaneously:

- Develop the two surveys based on collecting and correlating the data as accurately as possible.

- Collect Data: Gather employee experience ratings (e.g., job satisfaction, engagement, workplace culture) and customer experience ratings (e.g., satisfaction, Net Promoter Score, customer service feedback).

- Align Metrics: Ensure that both sets of ratings are measured on comparable scales. For example, if employee satisfaction is rated on a scale of 1-10, ensure that customer satisfaction is also on a similar scale.

- Analyse Trends: Use statistical methods (like correlation analysis) to see if higher employee satisfaction correlates with higher customer satisfaction. For instance, you might find that when employees rate their job satisfaction highly, customer satisfaction scores are also higher.

- Look for Patterns: Identify specific aspects where improvements in employee experience seem to impact on customer experience. For example, if employees report feeling more supported, it might coincide with improved customer service ratings.

- Consider External Factors: Consider other variables that could influence both employee and customer experiences, such as company policies, training programs, or market conditions.

- Draw Insights: Use the findings to understand how enhancing employee satisfaction could potentially lead to better customer experience and vice versa. For instance, a happy, engaged employee might deliver better customer service, leading to more satisfied customers.

HR Practice Note: Talent Management and Performance Solution

- Meet with line: Talent Management Discussion: Present the approach to
- be undertaken: Using Storytelling: Position HR and the advantages of using the approach; approach is where you are now concerning the problem and where you would I like to be once the problem is addressed.
- Conversation on the problem: (Where are you now?)
- Problem named, outlined: The current Talent Management System
- cumbersome and the results on the discussion outcomes are too late and are not aligned to the required succession decisions.
- Route course/s of problem noted and the impact it is having in the area:
- The 9-grid talent management system not user friendly and complex and conversations end where the names are placed into the boxes without further actions in practice. Conversation on various possible solutions (Where we need to be?) Conversation of all staff and where they are in terms of their career development, knowing what their strengths are and areas of development.
- Conversation of steps to get us to where we want to be once the problem is addressed (How are we going to get there?) We

have discussions with our talented staff members, we talk about their areas of development immediately and we talk to higher level positions and the person's readiness agility to move upwards. We talk about the training that the person would need to be advised to attend by their line manager and the timelines specified for the possibilities.

- *Theme name solution and cluster depending on the problem and categorisation of the people that it affects in the area. :3 Categories: (1.) Staff who need development and want stretch assignments (2) staff who prefer alternative working arrangements (3) staff who enjoy the fast pace and are ready for promotion. Implementation steps developed with timelines and responsible persons. Implementation Chart and schedule next meeting to determine Progress & & Impact of Implementation.*

HR Practice Note: HR Professional Practices of High Performance

- *Be proactive:* Winners anticipate problems before they arise as winners create

- *Prioritise:* master what truly matters: Either Delegate, Delete or schedule incomplete tasks

- *Set High Goals:* Be ruthless in setting your goals as these inspire and drive you. Review your goals constantly as these need to evolve for you to evolve

- *Network:* as opportunities are made in conversations, build relationships as doors will open when you least expect them

- *Be Optimistic* surround yourself with people who energise you and develop a practice of gratitude.

- *A lifetime of Learning:* Learning is not optional. Be open to feedback. Milk all successes and failures as an opportunity to learn from

- *Think beyond today:* Always be 10 steps ahead. Think about tomorrow like your life depends on it because it does

- *Own your wins,* losses and especially your own effort. If you make excuses, you will be regarded as an amateur.

HR Practice Note: HR/Sales Intervention

So, another example in practice is the collaboration with the sales team to increase sales through effective employee engagement intervention.

Increasing sales through an employee engagement intervention requires a thoughtful approach that aligns employee motivation, satisfaction, and productivity with business goals. Here is a structured way to go about it:

- **Assessment and Planning**

- **Evaluate Current Engagement Levels:** Conduct surveys or focus group sessions through interviews to understand how engaged your employees are currently. Identify factors influencing engagement and their impact on sales.

- **Set Clear Objectives:** Define specific sales targets or metrics you aim to improve through increased employee engagement.

- **Identify Key Engagement Drivers**

- **Employee Needs and Motivations:** Understand what motivates your employees beyond financial incentives (e.g., recognition, career growth, work-life balance). This identification needs to be done at the individual level as what motivates Anne is not what would motivate John.

- **Job Satisfaction:** Assess if employees have the necessary tools, resources, and support to perform their roles effectively.

- **Designing the Intervention**

- **Communication and Transparency:** Ensure clear and open communication about the goals of the intervention and how it aligns with company objectives. Sales and executive management need to be on board with this for consistency in communication by all stakeholders.

- **Training and Development:** Offer skill development opportunities that enhance both job performance and career growth. The type of skills required by salespersons is noted in the example further below.

- **Recognition and Rewards:** Implement effective recognition programs that acknowledge individual, and team achievements tied to sales performance.

- **Well-being Initiatives:** Promote work-life balance initiatives and support programmes that enhance overall employee well-being.

- **Implementation**

- **Leadership Buy-in:** Secure support from leadership to endorse and actively participate in engagement initiatives.

- *Engagement Activities:* Organise team-building exercises, workshops, or social gatherings and organisational events to foster a positive work environment.
- *Feedback Mechanisms:* Establish regular feedback loops to gauge employee sentiment and adjust strategies as needed.

- *Monitoring and Evaluation*

- *Performance Metrics:* Track sales performance metrics alongside engagement levels to measure impact.
- *Employee Feedback:* Continuously gather feedback to assess the effectiveness of the intervention and make necessary adjustments. This can be done on videos that can be filled with employees and how they feel about their own engagement levels within the company.

- *Continuous Improvement*

  - *Iterative Approach:* Use insights gained from monitoring and feedback to refine engagement strategies over time.
  - *Celebrating Success:* Recognise and celebrate milestones achieved through improved engagement and sales performance.

- *Sustainability*

- *Embedding Engagement:* Integrate employee engagement practices into your organisational culture to sustain long-term improvements in sales and overall business performance.

- By following these steps, you can create a holistic employee engagement intervention that not only boosts sales but also enhances employee satisfaction, productivity, and retention. Remember, sustained engagement requires ongoing commitment and adaptation to meet evolving employee needs and business goals.

HR Practice Note: Developing Key Sales Skills

Developing key sales skills in this intervention is crucial for maximising sales performance. Here are some essential sales skills that require focus within the training and development programmes that the HR Intervention would need to offer:

- **Communication Skills**

  - Active Listening: Ability to listen attentively to customer needs and understand their concerns.
  - Verbal Communication: Clear and persuasive verbal communication to convey product benefits and close deals effectively.
  - Non-verbal Communication: Awareness of body language and facial expressions to build rapport and convey trust.

- **Negotiation Skills**

  - Negotiation Techniques: Ability to negotiate terms, pricing, and agreements while maintaining positive relationships with customers.
  - Conflict Resolution: Skill in resolving objections and conflicts that arise during the sales process.

- **Product Knowledge**

  - Deep Understanding: Thorough knowledge of the products or services being sold, including features, benefits, and competitive advantages.

- Application Knowledge: Ability to demonstrate how products solve customer problems or fulfil specific needs.

- **Problem-Solving Skills**

  - Analytical Thinking: Capability to assess customer challenges and propose effective solutions.
  - Creativity: Ability to think innovatively to tailor solutions that meet unique customer requirements.

- **Relationship Building**

  - Building Rapport: Establishing and maintaining positive relationships with customers built on trust and mutual respect.
  - Customer Engagement: Engaging customers through personalised interactions and understanding their buying motivations.

- **Time Management**

  - Prioritisation: Effective management of time and resources to focus efforts on high-potential opportunities.
  - Efficiency: Streamlining the sales process to minimise downtime and maximise productivity.

- **Resilience and Persistence**

  - *Handling Rejection:* Ability to bounce back from rejection and maintain motivation throughout the sales cycle.
  - *Follow-up:* Persistence in following up with prospects to nurture relationships and close deals.

- **Adaptability**

  - *Flexibility:* Ability to adapt sales strategies and approaches based on customer feedback and market changes.
  - *Learning Agility:* Willingness to continuously learn and improve sales techniques in response to evolving customer needs and industry trends.

- **Closing Skills**

  - *Decision Making:* Guiding prospects through the decision-making process and effectively asking for the sale.
  - *Closing Techniques:* Mastery of various closing techniques to secure commitments from customers.

- **Technology Proficiency**

  - *CRM Systems:* Competence in using Customer Relationship Management (CRM) systems to track leads, manage pipelines, and analyse sales data.
  - *Digital Tools:* Utilisation of digital tools and platforms for prospecting, communication, and sales presentations.

Developing these key sales skills requires continuous practice, feedback, and learning. Sales professionals who excel in these areas are better equipped to build strong customer relationships, meet sales targets, and contribute to the overall success of their organisation. Examples of training programs and initiatives that HR might implement to support sales employees:

- **Sales Training Programs:**
    - Product Knowledge Training: Ensuring sales teams understand the features, benefits, and competitive advantages of products/services.
    - Sales Techniques and Strategies: Training on effective sales methodologies, objection handling, closing techniques, and relationship building.
    - Customer Persona Training: Teaching sales teams how to identify and understand customer personas to tailor their approach and messaging accordingly.
- **Professional Development Programs:**
    - Leadership Development: Training programs designed to develop leadership skills among sales managers and team leads.
    - Coaching and Mentoring: Pairing experienced sales professionals with newer team members to provide guidance and mentorship.

- o Time Management and Organisation: Training on prioritisation, time management techniques, and organisational skills to optimize productivity.

- **Technology and Tools Training:**
  - o CRM Training: Providing comprehensive training on using Customer Relationship Management (CRM) software effectively to track leads, manage pipelines, and enhance customer interactions.
  - o Sales Automation Tools: Training on tools that automate repetitive tasks, streamline workflows, and improve efficiency in the sales process.

- **Soft Skills Development:**
  - o Communication Skills: Workshops and exercises to improve verbal and written communication skills, including active listening and effective presentation techniques.
  - o Negotiation Skills: Training sessions on negotiation tactics, strategies, and best practices for achieving win-win outcomes in sales negotiations.

- **Industry and Market Training:**
  - o Market Intelligence: Providing insights into industry trends, competitor analysis, and market dynamics to help sales teams adapt their strategies.

- o Regulatory Training: Ensuring sales teams understand and comply with industry regulations, data privacy laws, and ethical standards.
- **Customer Service and Relationship Management:**
  - o Customer Experience Training: Teaching sales teams how to deliver exceptional customer service, handle customer inquiries, and resolve issues promptly.
  - o Building Long-Term Relationships: Training on strategies for building and maintaining long-term relationships with clients and stakeholders.
- **Cross-Functional Collaboration:**
  - o Team Building Workshops: Activities and exercises designed to promote teamwork, collaboration, and trust among sales team members and cross-functional teams.
  - o Interdepartmental Training: Training sessions that facilitate collaboration between sales, marketing, product development, and customer support teams to align strategies and goals.

These training programs and initiatives are designed to equip sales teams with the knowledge, skills, and tools they need to excel in their roles, contribute to organisational success, and adapt to the evolving demands of the marketplace.

HR plays a crucial role in supporting the sales team by ensuring they have the right talent through effective recruitment and hiring processes. HR also provides training and development programs to enhance sales skills and knowledge. They collaborate with sales managers to set performance goals and metrics, and design compensation packages that motivate and reward sales achievement. HR supports sales enablement with tools and resources, fosters employee engagement and retention, resolves conflicts, ensures compliance with regulations, and strategically aligns HR initiatives with sales strategies to drive organisational success.

HR Practice Note: Developing Skills to Champion the Implementation of the Great Employee Experiences

These practical examples tell you how you can improve, sharpen, enhance, and improve the employee experience:

- *Improving Employee Experience:*

  - *Conduct regular surveys to gather feedback from employees and implement changes based on their suggestions.*

  - *Offering comprehensive training and development programs to enhance skills and career growth opportunities.*

  - *Provide a supportive work environment where employees feel valued and respected.*

- *Sharpening the Employee Experience:*

  - *Implement personalised development plans for each employee tailored to their skills and career aspirations.*

  - *Offer mentorship programs to provide guidance and support for professional growth.*

  - *Provide regular constructive feedback to help employees refine their skills and performance.*

especially in team meetings and informal engagements

- *Enhancing Employee Experience:*

  - *Create a vibrant and inclusive workplace culture that promotes diversity and teamwork.*

  - *Offer flexible work arrangements to accommodate employees' needs and improve work-life balance.*

  - *Recognise and reward employees for their contributions through various incentives and recognition programs.*

- *Improving the Employee Experience through the key employee touchpoints:*

  - *Streamline HR processes such as onboarding, performance management, and benefits administration to reduce administrative burden on employees.*

  - *Implement technology solutions such as employee self-service portals to improve access to information and streamline communication.*

  - *Analyze employee data and metrics to identify areas for improvement and make data-driven* decisions to enhance the overall employee experience.

By incorporating these strategies, HR professionals can continuously improve, sharpen, enhance, and optimize the employee experience, leading to higher employee satisfaction, engagement, and retention and happier clients and greater profits.

HR Practice Note: General Satisfaction in The Work Environment : Pulse Survey Outcome :

Some Actionable Steps:

- **Conduct Stay Interviews**

  - **Rationale:** Stay interviews help identify what employees value most about their roles and what might cause them to leave.

  - **Value:** Proactively addressing concerns reduces turnover and improves retention, saving recruitment and training costs.

- **Recognise and Reward Contributions**

  - **Rationale:** Employees who feel appreciated are more motivated and engaged.

  - **Value:** Increased morale leads to higher productivity and a positive workplace culture.

- **Benchmark Satisfaction Scores**

  - **Rationale:** Comparing satisfaction scores with industry standards helps identify gaps.

  - **Value:** Ensures the company remains competitive in attracting and retaining talent.

Section 2: Work Environment

Actionable Steps:

- **Improve Collaboration Through Team Building**

  - **Rationale:** Stronger team relationships foster better communication and collaboration.

  - **Value:** Enhances teamwork, reduces conflicts, and improves project outcomes.

- **Create Safe Spaces for Feedback**

  - **Rationale:** Employees are more likely to share honest feedback when they feel safe.

  - **Value:** Identifies hidden issues and builds trust between employees and management.

- **Enhance Communication with Regular Updates**

  - **Rationale:** Transparent communication reduces uncertainty and aligns employees with company goals.

  - **Value:** Increases employee engagement and ensures everyone is working toward the same objectives.

Section 3: Management and Leadership

Actionable Steps:

Provide Leadership Training for Managers

- o **Rationale:** Skilled managers can better support, motivate, and guide their teams.

- o **Value:** Improves employee-manager relationships, leading to higher job satisfaction and performance.

- **Implement 360-Degree Feedback**

  - o **Rationale:** Feedback from peers, subordinates, and supervisors provides a holistic view of a manager's performance.

  - o **Value:** Helps managers identify blind spots and improve their leadership style.

- **Encourage Regular One-on-One Check-Ins**

  - o **Rationale:** Frequent conversations help address issues early and keep employees aligned with goals.

  - o **Value:** Builds trust, improves performance, and reduces misunderstandings.

Section 4: Career Growth and Development

Actionable Steps:

- **Create Personalized Development Plans**

  o **Rationale:** Employees are more engaged when they see a clear path for growth.

  o **Value:** Increases retention and prepares employees for future leadership roles.

- **Offer Training and Upskilling Programs**

  o **Rationale:** Continuous learning keeps employees updated with industry trends and skills.

  o **Value:** Enhances employee competence and innovation, benefiting the organisation.

- **Launch Mentorship Programs**

  o **Rationale:** Mentors provide guidance, support, and networking opportunities.

  o **Value:** Accelerates employee development and fosters a culture of learning.

Section 5: Work-Life Balance

Actionable Steps:

- **Introduce Flexible Work Arrangements**

  - **Rationale:** Flexibility helps employees manage personal and professional responsibilities.

  - **Value:** Reduces burnout, improves morale, and increases productivity.

- **Promote Well-Being Initiatives**

  - **Rationale:** Supporting mental and physical health leads to happier, healthier employees.

  - **Value:** Lowers absenteeism and healthcare costs while boosting engagement.

- **Encourage Time Off**

  - **Rationale:** Employees who take breaks are more productive and creative.

  - **Value:** Prevents burnout and maintains high performance levels.

Section 6: Compensation and Benefits

Actionable Steps:

- **Conduct Regular Salary Reviews**

  - **Rationale:** Competitive pay ensures employees feel valued and fairly compensated.

  - **Value:** Reduces turnover and attracts top talent.

- **Expand Benefits Offerings**

  - **Rationale:** Additional benefits (e.g., wellness programs, childcare support) address diverse employee needs.

  - **Value:** Enhances employee satisfaction and loyalty.

- **Communicate Pay Structures Transparently**

  - **Rationale:** Transparency builds trust and reduces perceptions of unfairness.

  - **Value:** Improves employee trust and reduces dissatisfaction.

Section 7: Company Culture

Actionable Steps:

- **Launch Diversity and Inclusion Initiatives**

  - **Rationale:** A diverse and inclusive workplace fosters innovation and belonging.

  - **Value:** Attracts diverse talent and improves team performance.

- **Celebrate Successes and Milestones**

  - **Rationale:** Recognising achievements boosts morale and reinforces positive behavior.

  - **Value:** Strengthens company culture and employee engagement.

- **Align Policies with Company Values**

  - **Rationale:** Consistency between values and actions builds credibility.

  - **Value:** Enhances employee trust and commitment to the organisation.

Section 8: Open-Ended Questions

Actionable Steps:

- **Analyze Feedback for Recurring Themes**

  - **Rationale:** Identifying common issues helps prioritize actionable changes.

  - **Value:** Addresses root causes of dissatisfaction and improves overall satisfaction.

- **Share Feedback and Action Plans with Employees**

  - **Rationale:** Transparency shows employees their feedback is valued and acted upon.

  - **Value:** Builds trust and encourages future participation in surveys.

- **Involve Employees in Solution Design**

  - **Rationale:** Employees feel more invested when they contribute to solutions.

  - **Value:** Increases buy-in and ensures solutions are practical and effective.

Overall Value to the Organisation:

- **Improved Retention:** Addressing employee concerns reduces turnover and associated costs.

- **Higher Productivity:** Engaged employees are more productive and innovative.

- **Stronger Employer Brand:** A positive workplace culture attracts top talent.

- **Better Decision-Making:** Employee feedback provides insights for strategic improvements.

- **Enhanced Employee Well-Being:** Supporting work-life balance and mental health leads to happier, healthier employees.

By implementing these actionable steps, HR professionals can create a more engaged, satisfied, and high-performing workforce, ultimately driving organisational success.

Improving employee satisfaction and engagement through the actionable steps outlined above can have a **direct and measurable impact on a company's bottom line and profitability.**

Here's how each recommendation connects to financial performance:

- **Improved Retention - Reduced Turnover Costs**

  - **Actionable Steps:** Conduct stay interviews, recognise and reward employees, and offer competitive compensation.

  - **Connection to Profitability:**

- o **Cost Savings:** Replacing an employee can cost **50-200% of their annual salary** due to recruitment, training, and lost productivity.

- o **Retention:** Satisfied employees are less likely to leave, reducing turnover costs and maintaining institutional knowledge.

- **Higher - Increased Productivity**

  - **Actionable Steps:** Improve collaboration, provide leadership training, and promote work-life balance.

  - **Connection to Profitability:**

    - o **Engaged Employees:** Engaged employees are **17% more productive** (Gallup).

    - o **Efficiency:** Better teamwork and communication reduce inefficiencies and errors, leading to faster project completion and higher-quality output.

- **Stronger Employer Brand through Enhanced Innovation and Creativity**

  - **Actionable Steps:** Create safe spaces for feedback, offer training programs, and launch mentorship initiatives.

- **Connection to Profitability:**

  - *Innovation:* Employees who feel valued and supported are more likely to contribute innovative ideas.

  - *Competitive Advantage:* New ideas can lead to improved products, services, or processes, driving revenue growth.

- **Enhanced Employee Well Being - Lower Absenteeism and Healthcare Costs**

  - **Actionable Steps:** Promote well-being initiatives, encourage time off, and offer flexible work arrangements.

  - **Connection to Profitability:**

    - *Reduced Absenteeism:* Healthy, balanced employees take fewer sick days.

    - *Lower Healthcare Costs:* Wellness programs can reduce healthcare expenses by preventing chronic illnesses and stress-related issues.

- **Improved Customer Satisfaction**

  - **Actionable Steps:** Train managers, align company values, and celebrate successes.

- **Connection to Profitability:**

  - **Employee-Customer Link:** Satisfied employees provide better customer service, leading to higher customer retention and loyalty.

  - **Revenue Growth:** Happy customers are more likely to make repeat purchases and recommend the company to others.

- **Attraction of Top Talent**

  - **Actionable Steps:** Benchmark satisfaction scores, expand benefits, and communicate transparent pay structures.

  - **Connection to Profitability:**

    - **Talent Acquisition:** A strong employer brand attracts high-performing candidates, reducing recruitment costs.

    - **Performance:** Top talent drives better business outcomes, such as increased sales or improved operational efficiency.

- **Stronger Company Culture and Alignment**

  - **Actionable Steps:** Launch diversity and inclusion initiatives, celebrate milestones, and align policies with values.

- **Connection to Profitability:**

  - **Employee Engagement:** A positive culture increases engagement, which is linked to **21% higher profitability** (Gallup).

  - **Alignment:** Employees who align with the company's mission and values are more committed to achieving organisational goals.

- **Data-Driven Decision Making**

  - **Actionable Steps:** Analyze feedback, share action plans, and involve employees in solution design.

  - **Connection to Profitability:**

    - **Targeted Improvements:** Addressing specific pain points improves efficiency and reduces wasted resources.

    - **Employee Buy-In:** Employees who feel heard are more likely to support changes, leading to smoother implementation and better results.

Quantifying the Impact

Here are some statistics that highlight the financial benefits of improving employee satisfaction:

- Companies with highly engaged teams see **21% higher profitability** (Gallup).

- Organisations with strong cultures of recognition have **31% lower voluntary turnover** (Bersin by Deloitte).

- A 5% increase in employee engagement can lead to a **3% increase in revenue growth** (Hay Group).

- Disengaged employees cost U.S. companies **450–550 billion annually** in lost productivity (Gallup).

Example Scenario

Imagine a mid-sized company with 500 employees and an average salary of $60,000. If the company reduces turnover by 10% through improved satisfaction initiatives:

- **Cost Savings:** Replacing 50 employees could cost $3 million (assuming 100% of annual salary per employee).

- **Productivity Gains:** Engaged employees could increase productivity by 17%, potentially adding millions in revenue.

- **Customer Retention:** *Improved customer service could increase repeat business, boosting revenue by 5-10%.*

*By investing in employee satisfaction, companies can achieve **tangible financial benefits**, including reduced costs, increased revenue, and improved profitability. These initiatives not only enhance the employee experience but also create a **competitive advantage** that drives long-term business success.*

HR Practice Note: How to Spot or Detect Signs of a Toxic Workplace Early

- If the language used by leaders is more to do with repercussions than growth, it is likely a fear driven culture

- If training or career development is not mentioned in the interviews, then there is probably no plan for it

- The respect for personal time is often reflected in boundaries that are set. Where emails for example are sent out late at night this means that employees are expected to always be available

- A lack of proper information is indicated where important updates catch employees by surprise. This is terrible communication as employees are often left in the dark as there is a little transparency on important decisions. And this makes it hard for teams to work together

- A lack of appreciation where leaders only talk about improvements and achievements are not celebrated. So hard work is not recognised and where employees have put in effort their contributions are rarely celebrated.

- Where promotions and decisions are influenced by favouritism than actual performance. Look for cliques at the office as office politics is likely at play and this creates an environment of who you know more matters rather than what you do.

- High staff turnover is signalled where staff leave often. Look at job boards to see if the same roles keep getting advertised. The company can't seem to keep its best people as questions are no longer being asked as its common knowledge that the best people are leaving

- Where leaders are involved in every little decision this indicates that they can't let go and that there is no trust. This results in people leaving the organisation. People will often want to protect themselves from toxic environments

HR Practice Note: Approach to Promoting HR

- **Develop Clear Messaging:** Communicate the benefits of HR services clearly and concisely, focusing on how they can solve problems and add value.

- **Create Engaging Content:** Use blogs, newsletters, webinars, or case studies to demonstrate thought leadership and expertise.

- **Leverage Internal Communication Channels:** Use internal emails, intranets, or meetings to inform employees and leadership about available HR services.

- **Engage with Stakeholders:** Build strong relationships with key leaders, managers, and employees to better understand their needs and promote services effectively.

- HR to **run monthly promotions** of their offering to give HR as much attention as possible. i.e. the attention of leadership and staff.

- Promoting HR's service offering so they know that HR exits in the company and that your magic works. In this way business would begin to build confidence and trust in HR. This would hopefully result in an improvement in the employee experience.

- **Offer Training and Resources:** Provide tools, workshops, or onboarding materials to ensure employees understand and utilise HR services.

- **Track and Measure Success:** Regularly assess the effectiveness of HR offerings through feedback, surveys, or performance metrics to make necessary improvements.

- **Use Technology:** Invest in HR software or platforms that can streamline service delivery and improve engagement.

- To **demonstrate the success of HR initiatives,** HR should collect and document feedback from both business leaders and employees regarding the successful implementation of HR solutions and interventions. HR will use its website to keep staff informed, regularly updating it with new reviews.

- In each **communication release, HR should include at least two to five reviews.** These releases should be hyperlinked to the corresponding reviews, corporate culture blogs, or shared via the company's internal social media channels.

- Employee engagement survey outcomes and the comparative analysis against other customer engagement metrics are an important results for HR and the Business as it gives HR its credibility in terms of its value add.

- So, in the promoting pillar of people to profit the HR professional needs to focus on :
  - Partnering
  - Pitching : Looking for all opportunities to present HR's Value add , interventions that have an impact to the business bottom-line
  - Performing : Demonstrating Return on Investment and business results through increased profits.

Where HR is able to demonstrate its value-add HR is to find more opportunities to :

- to speak and present,
- Consult
- Coach individuals and teams
- Connect with leadership of the business
- Actively participate in organisational strategic events and play an active role
- Look for opportunities to be provided with a bigger budget.

It's important for HR to also choose the right opportunities to speak at such as:

- Company Events
- Trade Shows
- Round table discussions
- HR Industry Forums and so forth.

At these opportunities Human Resource professionals are to also offer for eg:

- Free audio downloads on great leadership practice or any other empowering practice note or
- If they would like a coaching opportunity for themselves and their teams.
- Or create a segment that appeals to employees about loving their work environment and creating an environment that produces that by linking it to a key activity of the month .e.g. Valentines Day or Women's month and so forth.

By following these steps, HR professionals can successfully promote their services and align them with the organisation's goals.

General Best Practices for HR:

- **Communicate Progress:** Regularly update employees on the actions taken based on their feedback.
- **Measure Impact:** Conduct follow-up surveys to assess whether changes have improved satisfaction.
- **Foster a Feedback Culture:** Encourage continuous feedback and make it a part of the company's DNA.

By addressing these areas systematically, HR professionals can create a more engaged, satisfied, and productive workforce.

Point to Ponder: *What are some of the actionable steps that an HR Professional can recommend to further demonstrate HR's value add to their company bottomline? After correlating the Employee Satisfaction Survey outcomes with the outcomes of the company's client satisfaction survey?*

Before you go... *I just wanted to show appreciation and thanks for you purchasing this book. Now if you liked this book, please take a minute or two to leave a review so that other readers just like you can find out more about it. Your feedback will help me to continue writing books that get results.*

Call to Action: Take your HR expertise to the next level

Scan the below QR code *to gain access to expert-led, practical frameworks and a community of like-minded HR professionals. Don't just keep up, continue to lead the way in HR!*

www.ingramcontent.com/pod-product-compliance
Lightning Source LLC
Chambersburg PA
CBHW080514220326
41599CB00032B/6082